Wiring The Layout

Jeff Geary

KRB Publications
2 Denewulf Close
BISHOPS WALTHAM
Hants
SO32 1GZ

ISBN 0954203550

Printed by the Amadeus Press

Acknowledgements

The original suggestion for this book, and a great deal of encouragement since, came from Kevin Robertson, without whom it would not have been written. I am most grateful for Kevin's help and advice.

I should also like to express my thanks to my friends at the Winchester '0' Gauge Group, especially to John Shaw, who showed me how a layout ought to be operated, to David Yule, who loaned me much useful material on trackwork, and to Graham Hatton, who educated me in the way things are done in the real world. Graham works at 12 inches to the foot as well as 7mm.

Finally, to all those who have brought locomotives to run on the test track at the Winchester Group meetings, thanks a lot. Especial thanks to those whose engines have reversed the normal role of a test track. Our controller circuit would not have got where it is today without being regularly tested by your many 'difficult' locomotives!

I would also thank, John Shaw and Michael Ball for permission to use their photographs.

Jeff Geary, Whitchurch, 2002.

Contents

Introduction

Of all the many aspects to railway modelling, none attracts more misunderstanding, frustration and bewilderment than the 'electrics'. To many modellers, it is a black art, shrouded in mystery with its own strange language. To others, it is where the Gremlins live. Yet there has been remarkably little written on the subject. This book is an attempt, by one who has made plenty of wrong connections and learned much in the school of re–wiring the layout, to offer a few suggestions which may help to smooth the reader's path.

The book is accompanied by a CD–ROM which, for those readers who use an IBM–compatible PC, may prove to be of interest. It includes a program called Trax, which grew out of a number of small programmes I have written over the years to help with some aspects of layout wiring design and testing. It is by no means essential to have a PC in order to use the book, however. The text includes illustrations and explanations of all aspects covered by the program. The program will, however, enable to you to build a computer model of your own layout, then design and test its wiring a great deal more easily than by trial and error.

There are a great many ways to approach wiring a layout, and this book does not attempt to cover them all. I feel qualified only to offer advice on schemes with which I have direct experience, and these are fairly basic two–rail systems. However, I can claim to have built and used every circuit in the book at one time or another on a real layout or test track – they may not always have been suitable, but that's how we learn about circuit limitations!

Important Note

The Trax computer programme contained within this book is supplied as part of the book and CD ROM package. It is intended solely for the use of the purchaser and is not to be lend, hired, copied or stored in any other form other than as it is originally supplied. Whilst every care has been taken in the production of the programme, neither KRB Publications nor the author can accept any responsibility whatsoever for any damage caused by use of this programme. By opening the sealed package containing the CD ROM the purchaser agrees to accept these conditions.

Perfection in 12 inch to the foot scale. Trackwork at Bristol viewed from the West Signal Box and looking towards Bedminster.

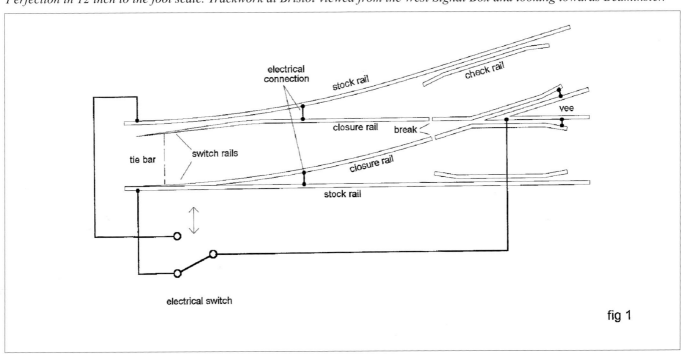

fig 1

Chapter 1

WIRING BASICS

In this chapter, we look at the process of developing a track plan for the model railway, and some of the basic principles of wiring it up. We shall be concerned exclusively with *two–rail operation*, where the two running rails are used to convey electrical power to the locomotive from a controller. There are other schemes, although none are as widely used. However, I have no personal experience of them, and it would therefore seem presumptuous to try to cover them.

Two–Rail Operation

A model railway train controller is provided with two output terminals, generally referred to as *live* and *return* and these are connected one to each of the running rails of the track at a point known as a *feed*. The use of the terms live and return has nothing to do with which of the terminals is at a positive or negative voltage, since this polarity will be reversed by changing controller's direction setting. However there are some conventions which you might find it useful to follow. If you follow the conventions, then you will not find that other peoples locomotives run backwards on your layout, which can be embarrassing!

Locomotives should be so wired that if you imagine yourself as the driver looking from the cab towards the front of the locomotive, then when the rail on your *right* is *positive*, the locomotive should move *forwards*. When the rail on your *left* is positive, the locomotive should move *backwards*.

When you wire your controller to a feed, you will obviously want to arrange matters so that the engine moves in the same direction as that of the arrow on the controller's direction switch when viewed from the normal operating position. If it does not, simply reverse the live and return connections to the controller. The current will then flow the opposite way through the engine's electric motor, and the direction of motion will be reversed.

In the case of a locomotive which has only one set of wheels insulated from the chassis and the other set live, it is conventional that the live wheels are on the left. This would be important, for example, if you were double–heading a train with two engines. If they had opposite wheel sets live, you might well get a short via their coupling hooks.

Pickups

One of the commonest sources of difficulty in achieving smooth operation of the railway lies in the transfer of power from rail to locomotive. The objective is to achieve an uninterrupted flow of current from the live rail, through the wheels, thence through the motor, back to the opposite–side wheels and back to the return rail. In practice, this is very difficult to achieve.

Any unevenness in the track may cause wheels to lift from the rail. At crossings, where the wheels have to jump the gap at the crossing nose, wheels can also lose contact. Dirt on the track or wheel can interrupt electrical continuity. You can keep both track and wheels clean by regular use of an abrasive block, or one of the liquid rail cleaners on the market.

Then there is the problem of picking up current from a rotating wheel. There are basically two approaches. The first involves wheels with insulated spokes and some sort of sliding contact with the wheel rim. This can either be via a strip of phosphor–bronze or a similar springy metal bearing upon the upper surface of the wheel tread, or by spring–loaded plunger pickups which bear upon the back of the wheel rim. The latter have the advantage of being easier to conceal. An alternative approach is to dispense with pickups entirely, use wheels with conducting spokes, and transfer power via the bush in which the axle runs. Obviously, this would require that the wheels on the other side were isolated by some sort of split axle arrangement. My own preference is to have electrically live wheels on the left of a steam locomotive, and have the live wheels on the right of the tender, the coupling between the two being electrically isolated from the locomotive chassis, and transferring power to the motor from the tender wheels. I do have the advantage, in this regard, of modelling a line on which tank engines were rarely seen, although I have successfully applied the scheme to an 0–4–4 tank engine, and to a Bo–Bo diesel, by grouping the wheels in fours, having the first group live on one side, the second on the other.

Points

Points allow us to switch a locomotive from one route to another. Fig 1 illustrates a typical point so that we can illustrate its main component parts. If you regard the point as looking rather like the side view of a foot, i.e. taller at the ankle end than at the toe, then you will have no trouble identifying the *heel* and *toe* ends, as they are called. At the toe end of the point, we have two *stock rails*. These are the fixed rails that extend the full length of the point on either side. Abutting these at the toe are the two *switch rails*. These are planed at the ends, and fit tight up against the stock rails in one position, and leave a gap wide enough to allow the wheel flange to pass between them and the stock rail in the other. They are moved together into one position or the other by one or more *tie bars*. The function of the switch rails, as their name implies, is to switch the train in one direction or another. In either direction, once it has passed the toe end of the switch rails, the train will run along one stock rail and one switch rail. At the heel end of the switch rails, the moveable part of the point ends, and the switch rails connect to the fixed *closure rails*.

As the train moves towards the heel end of the point, the divergence between the two directions becomes greater and greater. Eventually the two closure rails will need to cross each other. This is done by means of an *acute crossing*. At the nose of the crossing, the wheel needs to jump a small gap to reach the point rails, which make up the crossing vee itself. To ensure that the wheel chooses the right exit at this

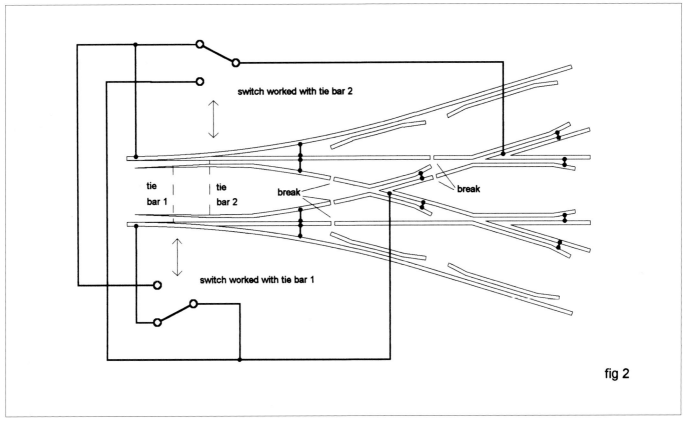

fig 2

gap, the *check rails* serve to pull the opposite wheel flange in the correct direction.

Now, if you think about two–rail operation, then when a locomotive enters a point at the toe end, and it is to be switched to the left, as in fig 1, we require the left hand stock rail to be negative, and the right hand stock, switch and closure rails to be positive. This will get our locomotive up to the crossing vee. Here, we will cross the vee with the right hand wheels, so we want these to be positive – i.e. the same polarity as the right hand stock rail. Now consider what happens if the locomotive is to be switched to the right. Again, we want the right hand stock rail to be positive, and the left hand stock, switch and closure rails are all to be negative. This time, however, when we get to the crossing vee, this will be crossed by the left hand set of wheels, so we now want it to be negative – i.e. the same polarity as the left hand stock rail.

Thus, in addition to moving the switch rails by means of the tie bar(s), we need

some method of switching the polarity of the crossing vee. If you use proprietary points you will generally find that there is a switch mechanism built into the point. If you make your own track, it is necessary to build this switch into the circuit of the layout somewhere. Ideally, it should be combined with the mechanism used to operate the point switch rails.

Conventionally, the electrical feed to points should always be to the two stock rails at the toe end. The switch and closure rails are electrically connected to their adjacent stock rails, and the crossing vee is switched from one stock rail to the other.

Three–way Points

A *three–way point* involves three acute crossings, and two pairs of switch rails linked by tie–bars. The point has, as its name implies, three exits. In fig 2 if both tie bars are to the left (as viewed from the toe end) the train will take the right hand exit. If both tie bars are to the right the train will take the left hand exit. If one tie

bar is left and one right (as drawn), the train will go straight on. The benefit of a three way point is that it saves a great deal of space. The same result could be acheived with a left and right hand point in tandem, but at the cost of doubling the length.

As with the two–way point, wiring is necessary to ensure that the crossing vees have the correct polarity for a given setting of the switch rails. Although there are three crossing vees, not all possible combinations of polarity are required. We can therefore have the central crossing vee electrically continuous with one of the outer vees, and switch the polarity of the outer vees only. This considerably simplifies the wiring task.

Referring again to fig 2, you will see that power is fed into the point at the toe end, as before, and two separate electrical switches are used to change the polarity of the crossing vees. As with two–way points, these can be built into the mechanism used to operate the points. Three way points are generally operated with two levers, so this is not a problem. Caution is required operating three–way points. If you note which switch blades are operated by which tie–bars, you will see that there is one setting (the one where both switches in fig 2 are reversed) which is physically impossible. Of course if force is used to try to set them, damage could result. A means of preventing this is mentioned in chapter 4.

At the present time, Trax does not include a three–way point facility. From the electrical point of view, however, the combination of a left and right hand point in tandem is equivalent. By choosing points with very short switch rails and very large crossing angles, you can compress the combination to the point where it occupies little more space than a more gracefully curved three–way point. It is hoped that in a future version, three way points will be included.

Diamond Crossings

A *diamond crossing*, unlike a point, has no moving parts. It simply allows one track to cross another. However, we still need to change the polarity of the acute crossing vees. Referring to fig 3, if we are going from A to C, then the first crossing vee will be traversed by the right hand wheels, and will thus require to be positive, and the second crossing vee will be traversed by the left hand wheels and will thus require to be negative. If we are going from B to D, then the left hand wheels are on the first crossing vee and the right hand ones on the second, so polarities must be reversed. In between the two crossing vees are what are known as the *obtuse crossings*, and their component parts, the *point rails*, *elbow rail* and *obtuse check rail* are also shown. Now, if we wish to go from A to C or from B to D, we will always encounter the upper elbow rail with our left hand wheels, and the lower elbow rail with our right. Thus these polarities must not change.

We therefore need to switch the polarities of the acute crossings,

depending on which way we are intending to drive our locomotive over the diamond crossing. Unfortunately, this is rather less convenient than with points. Because a diamond has no moving parts, we cannot simply incorporate the polarity switch into the mechanism for setting the direction.

On occasions, you may find that the track plan allows you to conceal the switching of diamond crossing polarity into the switching of the points feeding the diamond (there is an example of this described later). In other cases, you will be able to build the polarity switching into the operation of nearby signals. However, in the worst case, you will need a double pole switch to handle the polarity change, as shown in the figure.

Double Slips

A *double slip* is a development from the diamond crossing in which each of the incoming tracks to the diamond is equipped with a pair of switch rails such that it can take *either* of the two exit tracks

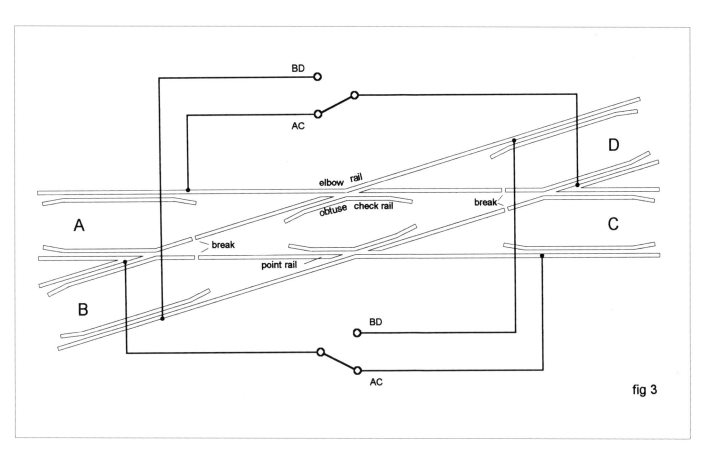

fig 3

on the opposite side of the diamond. A double slip therefore has no less than four pairs of switch rails, two acute crossings and two obtuse crossings. As with the diamond, the essential requirement is to switch the polarity of the two acute crossings according to the tracks on which the train enters and leaves the formation.

Fortunately, as with the three–way point, not all possible combinations are required, so the wiring can be somewhat simpler than you might expect, given the complexity of the track formation. It is the setting of the switch on the 'entry' side of the double slip that determines which track the train will exit on. Referring to fig 4, if the train enters at A, the setting of switch rails 1a will decide which way it goes (i.e. to C or D). The setting of switch rails 1b is irrelevant. Therefore, we can drive both tie–bars 1a and 1b from the same lever, and similarly at the other end.

The polarity of the acute crossings at either end of the double slip must be switched according to the route to be taken. Recall that it is the switch rails on the entry side that determine which exit is to be taken. Therefore, the switch rail setting on the entry side will determine what polarity is required on the acute crossing on the exit side. Thus each pair of tie–bars operate the electrical switching of the *opposite* crossing vee.

As we have seen, the recommended method of wiring points is to feed power in at the toe of the point, and never at the heel end (i.e. where the acute crossing is). However, the double slip has a 'heel' at both ends. Therefore, power is generally fed to a double slip at the two elbow rails in the centre of the crossing. The switches at each then feed this power to the acute crossings as required.

Single Slips

The *single slip*, like the double slip, is derived from the diamond crossing. As its name implies, however, it has only a single set of switches at each end. Referring to fig 5, a train entering at A can be switched to either of the two exits C or D. However, a train entering at B can only exit at D. Similarly, a train entering at D could exit at A or B, but one entering at C could only exit at A.

You might think that wiring a single slip would be easier than wiring a double slip, but unfortunately this is not so. With a double slip, all four combinations of the two pairs of tie–bars lead to valid routes through the slip (i.e. A to C, A to D, B to C, B to D and their opposite routes). However, with a single slip, only three of the four combinations lead to valid routes (B to C, and its opposite, C to B, being invalid). Care must be taken to avoid setting this route.

The wiring is in principle exactly the same as for a double slip, with the switch tie–bar at each end determining the polarity of the acute crossing at the opposite end. Power is again fed into the elbow at the centre of the crossing.

A picture, they say, is worth a thousand

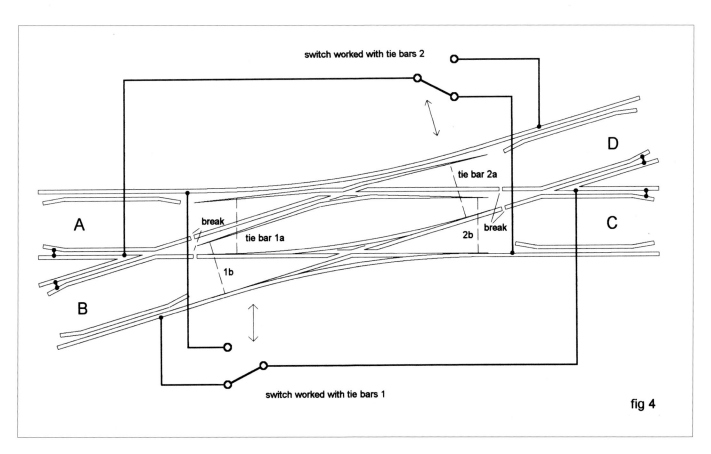

fig 4

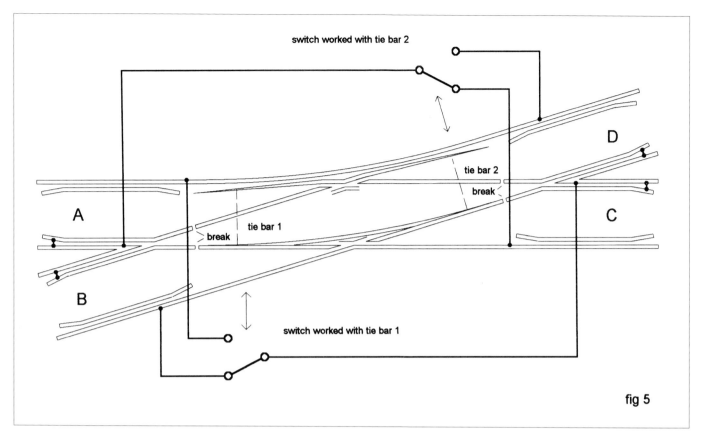

switch worked with tie bar 2

D

tie bar 2

break

A

tie bar 1

break

C

B

switch worked with tie bar 1

fig 5

words. However, when it comes to switching crossing vee polarities, a moving picture is worth two thousand words! If you are using the Trax program, you may find it helpful to load the program, and then open the example file named 'diamond slips.trx'. This contains a diamond and single and double slips. If you right click on each of them in turn and select 'properties' you will observe that their settings are changed by the switches s1 ... s5. Click the 'Test/Operate' button (the little green arrow) or select Tools|Test Layout, then experiment with these switches to observe the route selection through the crossings. Turn off the Show Track Single option to look at the colour–coded polarity of the individual crossings being switched.

Track Feeds and Breaks

The simplest possible model railway layout would require only one controller and a single track feed. All switching of power to different parts of the track

would be handled by the same mechanism as that which handles the switching of polarity to point crossings. Some layouts are, in fact, this straightforward. Essentially what is required is to find a location for the feed from which, by an appropriate initial setting of the points and crossings every other possible location could be reached by a train without having to make any further changes to point settings.

If such a location can be found, a track feed can be placed here, a single controller connected to it, and the layout will run perfectly well. Because there is only one controller of course, only one locomotive can run at a time. However, more than one locomotive could be on the layout, those not required to run being isolated on parts of the layout not selected by the point settings at any one time.

However, in many cases, it will be found that there are parts of the layout that require a locomotive to move from the feed location to an intermediate location

on the track, then a point must be changed *before* the train can reach the desired destination. In all such cases, it will be found that more than one track feed is required.

Generally speaking, if there is more than one feed to a layout, it will be necessary to locate a track break between the two feed positions. This is because one of the feeds will, in all likelihood, be feeding into the 'heel' end of a point. When the point is set the 'wrong' way, this will cause a short circuit. Therefore, a suitably placed track break must be incorporated. A track break is best made after the track has been laid, either with a piercing saw or a slitting disc in a minidrill. It is a good idea to pack the gap thus left with araldite or similar to prevent accidental bridging of the gap.

There are other situations where track breaks are essential to prevent short–circuits. The most common is that of a point leading off a circle or oval. If the circle or oval is continuous, then when the

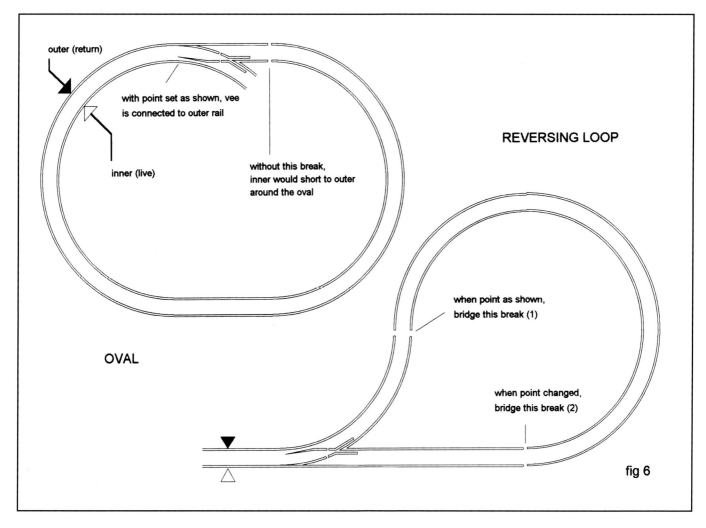

outer (return)

with point set as shown, vee
is connected to outer rail

REVERSING LOOP

inner (live)

without this break,
inner would short to outer
around the oval

when point as shown,
bridge this break (1)

OVAL

when point changed,
bridge this break (2)

fig 6

point is changed to the diverging line a short–circuit will occur unless the circle or oval contains a track break. In a *reversing loop*, there must be two breaks, moreover the section between them must have its polarity reversed when the point controlling entry to the loop changes. Fig 6 shows these situations. In the reversing loop case, the breaks are bridged, that labelled break 1 being bridged if the point is set left and that labelled break 2 being bridged if the point is set right.

Multiple Controllers

On larger layouts, it will be possible to run several trains at once, using multiple controllers. The presence of several controllers makes for some additional requirements in terms of track

feeds and breaks. You will need to decide first of all on your operating strategy.

Your layout may break down into logical sections, for example in a layout based on a double track oval or circle, it might make sense to designate one line the up line, the other one the down line, and to have 'up' and 'down' controllers for the two main lines, with possibly a third controller to handle shunting in a goods yard. In such a case, the approach should be to first decide on what are the areas to be covered by a given controller, i.e. its *scope*. Then, look at each area in turn and decide how many feeds it needs from its 'own' controller (along the lines discussed above), and where these should be sited. Then, identify where trains may be required to pass from the

scope of one controller to another. There will need to be breaks in the track at these points, and arrangements must be made for allowing the controller into whose scope the train is moving to temporarily gain control over the controller whose scope the train is leaving. The ways we can do this are discussed later in the book.

Sometimes, the layout may not be amenable to this approach. For example, if the main line were a single track, then the concept of an 'up' and a 'down' controller would not be applicable. We might still, however, want to use two controllers. For example, the single line might have a station at one end, and either a second station or a fiddle yard at the other, and we might want to do some shunting at both locations. An approach often adopted here is that the operator who is going to *stop* the train *drives* it. Generally, this means the train will be driven by the operator who will be closest to the point where the train is to stop. More judgement is required to be exercised in stopping a train at the correct place than in starting it, so it makes sense to arrange matters this way round. In this case, the feeds on the single track line will need to be switched to one controller or another, depending on which way the train is going.

Use of Signals

As a layout becomes more complicated, especially if multiple controllers are involved, the need for special switching arrangements grows. A point is reached where it can become difficult to remember which switches have to be set for which routes/controllers. A far preferable scheme is to adopt a principle introduced to me by John Shaw's inspirational Aveton Gifford layout. This is, that so far as possible, *all* track circuitry should be controlled by points and signals. Ideally, the only electrical switch on a control panel should be the one that turns the station lights on and off. All feeds, track breaks, crossing polarity switches etc. should be controlled from a lever frame, as in a full–size signal box.

Additionally, the lever frame should have a clearly labelled diagram of the layout showing which levers control which points and signals, and the points should be drawn, as in full–size practice, shown in the position corresponding to their lever being in the normal position. (Levers in a lever frame are referred to as being *normal* or *reversed*, if the signalman has pulled them back). A number of manufacturers supply kits to build your own lever frame. Alternatively, you could in fact use a row of toggle switches as your 'lever frame'.

The benefits of this approach are: that it corresponds with full–size practice, always a good thing; that it is very clear from the track plan and the position of levers (or switches if used as such) which points and signals are reversed, and therefore which route is set; and finally that even an operator who cannot see the control panel in question should be able to see the signals on the layout and thereby should also know what route is set.

The aim of this book, therefore, is to show how to design the wiring arrangements for a railway layout such that this goal can be achieved. We wish to cater for the whole range of possible train movements that would be allowed in full–size practice, having all of the electrical switching happen 'behind the scenes' as it were, by virtue of the correct route having been set and signalled.

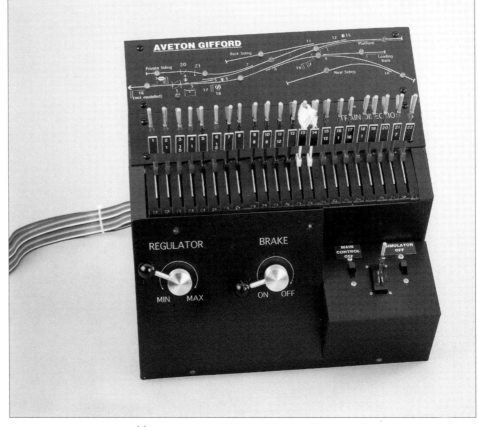

The lever frame from John Shaw's 'O' Gauge layout, 'Aveton Gifford'. Care in design and construction has resulted in both a reliable and realistic looking frame complete with mechanical interlocking. On the diagram the layout is split into various track sections and which when activated supplies both power to the track and illuminates an LED. The activation of each signal lever – coloured red in practice, operates a 4–pole changeover relay which in turn feeds two other relays, one in rear of and the other in front of the signal. The signal also selects which controller is to power the sections concerned. A separate 'King' lever on the lower right, is used to feed sidings for shunting and which are not signal controlled. To avoid the risk of collisions this can only be activated when all the signal levers are at 'normal' in the frame. Notice also the 'duster' on the levers!

Above:

Full size electrification – Southern style and the principles are just the same. A somewhat unusual view of one of the first pair of Bulleid–Raworth electric locos complete with its pantograph raised.

Left:

'A3' 2558 'Tracery' – tractive effort in 'Gresleys'? – see opposite page! What on earth then would have been measured in Bulleids....?

Chapter 2

THE PRINCIPLES OF ELECTRICITY

In the previous chapter, we used the terms voltage, current and power without really defining them, which was somewhat remiss although far from unusual. There is widespread confusion over exactly what these terms mean, and it is partly for this reason that many modellers despair of understanding how electrical circuits work. The intention of this chapter is to describe the fundamental concepts of current, voltage, charge and power and to introduce a few very simple formulae which relate them to each other. This will then enable us to introduce a number of electronic components and electromechanical devices, useful to modellers, and explain in outline how they work.

What is Electricity?

Electricity is associated with the *flow* of tiny charged particles called *electrons*. *Charge* comes in two flavours, which we call *positive* and *negative*. The only thing you really need to know about charge is this: *opposite charges attract, like charges repel*. Every electron possesses a tiny, fixed amount of negative charge. Therefore, electrons repel each other. Most of the electrons in nearly all substances are pretty tightly held inside atoms by the attraction of positively charged particles. However, in certain materials, principally metals, a few of the electrons are relatively free to move about. These materials are called *conductors* – they include copper, steel, brass and nickel–silver. Materials in which all the electrons are tightly bound up inside atoms and molecules are called *insulators*, and include plastics, paper, wood and so on.

Charge, Current and Voltage

This whole area is fraught with far more confusion than it deserves. By historical misfortune, the flow of electric current was discovered over a century before the discovery of the electron which carries it. The early pioneers, knowing nothing of the electron, made the assumption that electricity was carried by positive charges that flowed from the positive terminal of a circuit around to the negative. They had a fifty percent chance of being right, but sadly, the whole theory was well established before it was discovered that electricity was actually carried by negative charges going the other way! We are thus left with the unfortunate result that by convention, current flows from positive to negative, whilst in reality electron flow is from negative to positive. Much of the difficulty in talking about electrical and electronic devices stems from this mishap.

It is as if we were trying to describe what happens at the end of a film in the cinema, without mentioning the audience. Instead of saying 'people leave' we are, in effect, saying 'emptiness flows in through the doors and onto the seats'! What physically happens in electrical circuits is that *electrons* flow from *negative* to *positive*. By defining 'current' as flowing from positive to negative, the early pioneers raised a barrier to understanding electricity which is still there two centuries later!

There is a second source of difficulty, which is that instead of naming the units of current, charge and so on according to what they physically represent, they are named after the worthy Messrs Ampere, Volta, Watt, Coulomb and Ohm. In one sense this is rather charming, and was perhaps a missed opportunity by the railway community. We could have measured boiler pressures in Staniers or tractive effort in Gresleys! However, whilst many people are confused by the concept of an ampere, I am sure they would be less so if we talked about a rate of flow of electrons. We can measure rates of flow of water and gas through pipes in gallons per minute or cubic feet per second. An ampere is nothing more complicated than a certain number of electrons per second flowing through a conductor. If we could collect these electrons in a bucket, then the number we would collect (corresponding to total charge) in a given time would be the rate of flow (current) multiplied by time,

Charge = Current multiplied by Time

Conventionally, we use the symbol Q for charge, I for current and t for time, so the above can be briefly written as

$$Q = It$$

We measure charge in coulombs, after Charles Augustin de Coulomb who discovered the law of attraction and repulsion between charges. We can therefore say,

Coulombs
= Amperes multiplied by seconds

An ampere is thus a rate of flow of one coulomb per second, a coulomb being the charge on about six million million million electrons. An ampere is actually quite a large current. We are often concerned with much smaller ones, so we introduce the milliampere, often shortened to milliamp or abbreviated to mA, which is one thousandth of an ampere. Amperes are often shortened to amps, or abbreviated A.

Electrons, even in conductors, will not spontaneously set up a current since in general they will be moving around at random. Remember they repel each other, so they spend their time rushing to and fro trying (unsuccessfully) to get away from each other. There is no overall flow from one place to another, hence no current.

The purpose of a power source, such as a battery or a generator, is to use either chemical or mechanical means to force a large number of electrons from one location (called the positive terminal) to another (called the negative terminal). The electrons don't like being in crowds, and are keen to get away from each other. This sets up, in effect, a pressure tending to push electrons out of the negative terminal. Therefore, when you connect a conductor between the negative terminal and the positive, the electrons flow through it. The pressure pushing the electrons out of the negative terminal is what we measure as a *voltage*. A higher voltage, means nothing more than a greater pressure on the

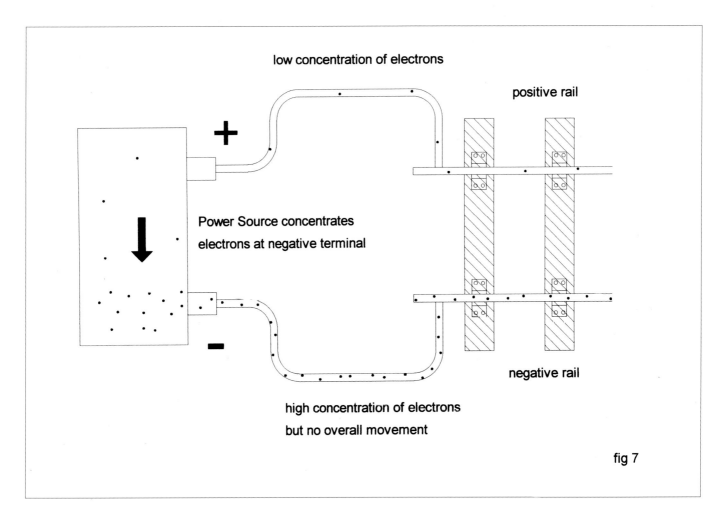

low concentration of electrons

positive rail

Power Source concentrates
electrons at negative terminal

high concentration of electrons
but no overall movement

negative rail

fig 7

electrons at the negative terminal.

Now, if you didn't before, you can very easily understand how you can have a large voltage, but no current. If you take a piece of plain railway track, and wire up the rails to the positive and negative terminals of a power supply, what will happen is this. Electrons will, very briefly, flow from the negative terminal onto one rail of the track. There they will stop. You can picture them all gathered on the negative rail, looking longingly over to the positive rail, but unable to get there as the sleepers are insulators and there is no way through. The current will flow only briefly, because very soon there will be just as high a concentration of electrons on the negative rail as at the negative terminal of the battery, so the pressures balance out. We now have a voltage across the rails, but no current. See fig 7.

Suppose we now stand a locomotive on the track. The electrons in the 'negative' rail now have a path over to the positive. Cheerfully, they rush through the locomotive's wheels, through its motor (and in doing so set up a mechanical force to turn the motor, but we'll come back to that), out through the wheels on the opposite side, and through the wire to the positive terminal. Once there, they are forced by the action of the battery or power supply circuit (again, we'll come back to this) back to the negative terminal, where they are ready to do the circuit again. We have a *current*.

If the pressure, or voltage, of the power source is a high one, the electrons will go round quickly so we will have a high rate of flow, or a large current. If the voltage is low, the pressure is not so great, and the

electrons will drift around more slowly, a smaller current will flow.

How much current will flow, for a given applied voltage? The answer lies in how easy a trip the electrons have. If they flow through excellent conductors, such as copper, their journey will be easy, they will do it quickly, and a large current will flow. If they have to flow through a poor conductor, their journey will be more difficult, and even with a large applied voltage, the current may only be small. A useful analogy would be to liken current to the rate of flow of traffic along a stretch of road. If the road is a good one, such as a wide motorway, traffic will flow easily. If the road is a narrow country lane, then traffic can only flow at a trickle.

We call this property of conductors their *resistance* to the flow of current. If a conductor needs a high voltage to get a given current to flow through it, we say it has a high resistance. If only a low voltage is required to get the same current flowing, we say that it has a low resistance. There is a very simple formula which connects voltage, current and resistance:

Voltage =
Current multiplied by Resistance

Remembering that the symbol I is conventionally used for current, and introducing V for voltage and R for resistance, the above can be written as:

$V = IR$

This is known as Ohm's Law (after Georg Ohm, a German electrical pioneer). If a conductor allows one amp of current to flow through it, given the application of one volt, then we say its resistance is one ohm. This gives us an alternative way of stating Ohm's law:

volts = amps multiplied by ohms

Resistors

Good conductors have very low resistances, typically only a fraction of an ohm. However, there are circumstances in which we want to restrict the flow of current and here we can employ an electronic component called a *resistor*. Resistors come in a variety of shapes and sizes, but in the main they are cylindrical with a connecting wire at each end. They are represented on a circuit diagram by a zig–zag line as in fig 8(a), usually with their resistance value written alongside.

Resistors can be obtained with resistance values as low as 0.1 ohm, and as high as 100,000,000 ohms or more. To save writing such large numbers of zeroes, we use the kilohm (1,000 ohms), usually abbreviated to k, and the megohm (1,000,000 ohms) abbreviated to M. Thus a resistor with a value of 4,700 ohms could be described alternatively as 4.7k. It is conventional to save yet more writing by making the 'k' (or 'M' for megohms) double up as the decimal point. Thus 4.7k is conventionally written as 4k7. Resistor values below 1,000 ohms are written with the letter R after them, thus 220R. With low values of resistance, the 'R' is again used to indicate the position of the decimal point, so 4R7 represents 4.7 ohms.

Large–size resistors generally have their value written on them, as 22R, 1k0, etc. However, on the smaller varieties there is insufficient space to allow legible labelling. On these, a colour–coding system is used, details of which appear in the Appendix.

All resistors obey Ohm's law. For example if you placed a 12v supply across a 1 kilohm resistor, the current through it would be 12/1000 = 0.012A or 12 mA

Potentiometers

What we have described so far are known as *fixed resistors*. They have two terminals with a fixed value of resistance between them. An important development from these is the *potentiometer*, which has three terminals. The upper and lower ones are connected to the ends of a fixed resistor, which takes the form of a curved track of resistive material. The third terminal is a wiping contact, arranged on a rotating spindle such that at one end of its travel it is at the lower end–stop of the fixed track, as the spindle turns it moves round the track, eventually making contact with the upper end–stop at the other end of its travel.

If we apply +12v to the 'upper' end of the potentiometer's track, and zero to the 'lower' end, then with the wiper at the end–stops, the voltage at the third terminal

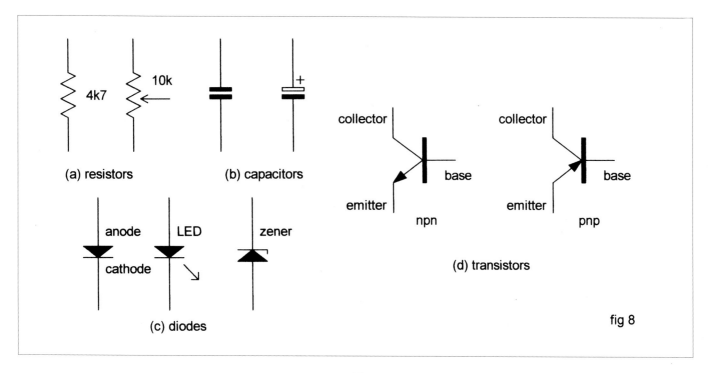

(a) resistors   4k7   10k

(b) capacitors

(c) diodes   anode   cathode   LED   zener

(d) transistors   collector   base   emitter   npn   collector   base   emitter   pnp

fig 8

will be 0 or +12v. If we positioned it halfway, the third terminal would be at +6v, a quarter of the way up it would be at +3v, and so on. A potentiometer is therefore used to obtain a continuously variable voltage from a fixed one.

Before we leave resistors, we should introduce the concept of *Power*. Power is measured in watts, after James Watt of steam engine fame, and is defined as the rate of doing work. In the electrical world, power has a very simple formula :

Power = Current multiplied by Voltage

or,

watts = amps multiplied by volts

Power is generally represented by the letter P, so remembering that I is used for current, and V for voltage, the above can be written as

$$P = IV$$

Another useful form of this formula is obtained by substituting the voltage using Ohm's law, remember: $V = IR$, so we also can say,

$$P = I^2R$$

Power in electrical devices can be used to do useful mechanical work (as in electric motors) or it can simply heat up the device. This might be exactly what we want, if the device is the element of an electric fire, but all too often, as in resistors for example, the heat is generally an unwanted by–product. Heating of resistors can be quite severe, and they can easily reach temperatures at which they start to disintegrate, often with a fairly acrid smell and more than a whisp of smoke! It is important, therefore, to ensure that any resistors we use are well within their Power Rating. This is generally expressed in Watts, and it represents the maximum power that the resistor can safely dissipate without self–destructing.

Typical small resistors come in 0.25 or 0.6W ratings, larger ones can be 1W, 3W, 5W or more. The main deciding factor in the power rating of a resistor is its ability to get rid of heat into the surrounding air. In general, this is dependent on surface area, so higher

power resistors are made with larger packages. Very high power resistors (25W plus) will often have metal fins to help them radiate heat.

Capacitors

We have already said that it is very difficult to collect a large number of electrons together in one place, because they tend to repel each other. The *capacitor* is a clever device in which a large number of electrons can be gathered together. This is done by collecting a similar number of positive charges, and using the attractive forces between positive and negative to balance the repulsive ones. Basically, a capacitor consists of two thin films of conductor (called the 'plates') with an insulating layer between them. When the capacitor is connected to a supply, electrons will leave the 'positive' plate and make their way to the positive terminal of the supply. This will leave the positive plate with a shortage of electrons. It will therefore have a positive net electrical charge. Electrons will leave the negative terminal of the supply, and be attracted towards the positive charge on the positive plate of the capacitor. They will not, however, be able to get there, because of the insulating layer. They will therefore accumulate on the negative plate of the capacitor, as close as they can get to the attracting positive charge, but unable to reach it. This process cannot go on for ever, of course, because the accumulation of electrons on the negative plate will start to build up a negative charge which will repel further additions. Very quickly, therefore, the capacitor will reach a state of equilibrium, which we describe as being fully charged. No further electrons will flow, and the charges on the capacitor's plates will be balanced. In effect, the capacitor is exactly like the length of rail in fig 7, although it has a far greater capacity to store electrons.

We could now, if we wanted, disconnect the capacitor from the supply and take it away. Its plates will still have their

accumulations of charge, which they will maintain almost indefinitely. This unique ability of the capacitor to store charge is called its *capacitance*, and is measured in farads, after Michael Faraday. If the application of one volt to the capacitor's plates is sufficient to enable it to store one coulomb of charge, then we say that its capacitance is one farad:

Charge
= Capacitance multiplied by Voltage
or
coulombs = farads multiplied by volts

Recall that we use Q as the symbol for charge, and introducing C for capacitance the above becomes

$$Q = CV$$

The capacitance of a capacitor depends on the area of its plates (larger plates can hold more electrons before they start repelling each other), and the thinness of the insulating layer between them (a thinner layer increases the 'attractiveness' of the positive plate and encourages more electrons onto the negative one). Practical capacitors generally have capacitances much less than one farad. We therefore commonly use the microfarad (abbreviated to µF), which is one millionth of a farad.

If we were to pursue our analogy relating electrical quantities to traffic, we might liken a capacitor to a large car park. Traffic would flow into the car park until it held as many cars as it could, and the flow would then cease. The analogy is not quite perfect, however, because whereas the capacity of a car park is a fixed number of cars, the capacitor could hold more charge if the applied voltage were to be increased.

The applied voltage could not be increased indefinitely, however, because at some point the insulating layer would break down. In large capacitors, this could give rise to quite a loud bang, together with sparks, smoke and flying debris! To avoid such mishaps, capacitors are labelled with a *maximum working voltage*, generally abbreviated to WV. You should never apply a voltage greater than this.

Some capacitors, especially large

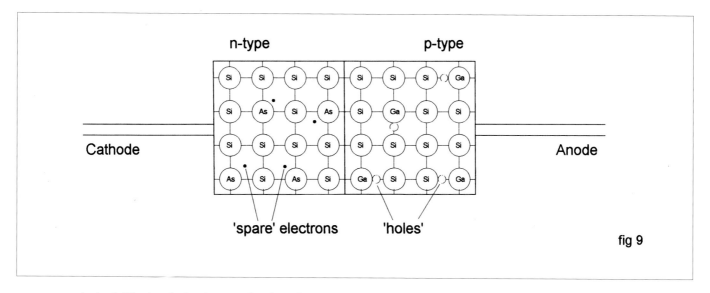

n-type · p-type

Cathode · Anode

'spare' electrons · 'holes'

fig 9

ones, are polarised. The insulating layer works only in one direction, so the applied voltage must always have the positive terminal connected to the positive plate of the capacitor, and the negative to negative. Failure to observe this precaution will also result in loud bangs! Fig 8(b) – page 15, shows how capacitors (both polarised and non–polarised) are represented on circuit diagrams.

Diodes

We discussed earlier how in insulators, the electrons are all held either tightly inside atoms, or are fully employed linking atoms together. None are therefore free to move around, so it is very difficult to pass an electric current through them. By contrast, good conductors, such as copper, have electrons which are held only very loosely by their parent atoms, and are not required to do any linking up with other atoms. We come now to an extremely useful group of substances which lie between the two, and are known as *semiconductors*. The most important of these are based on the element silicon. (Do not, by the way, make the common mistake of putting an e on the end. *Silicones*, which are man–made compounds, are completely different substances used in furniture polishes, lubricants and breast

implants!)

Silicon is poor conductor, about 50,000 times less effective at conducting electricity than copper. This is because, in a crystal of pure silicon, each atom's innermost electrons are very tightly held within the atom, and all of its four outermost electrons are used in linking the atom to its four neighbours in the crystal structure. There are therefore no electrons available to carry current. However, silicon's conductivity can be greatly increased by the addition of small and very carefully controlled amounts of impurities. For example, we could add a small amount of arsenic. Now, the arsenic atom has five electrons in its outermost layer. It is otherwise very similar to silicon, and can readily fit itself into the structure of the silicon crystal. In doing so, it uses only four of its five available electrons, leaving one for conduction. We now have an *n–type semiconductor*, n referring to the fact that the conductivity has been produced by the additional (negatively charged) electron.

We could alternatively increase silicon's conductivity by adding a material such as gallium. Gallium has only three outer electrons, and although it can equally well be incorporated into a silicon crystal, it does so leaving a 'hole' where its fourth electron (if it had one) would link up with an adjacent silicon atom. Now it might seem a bit

strange but this 'hole' is in effect a positive charge, and it too is able to move around the crystal. In reality, what happens is that an electron from an adjacent silicon atom can jump into the hole, thereby filling it, but leaving a new hole behind. These 'holes' are just as good as electrons at conducting electricity – the only difference is that the hole moves towards the negative voltage. This material is called a *p–type semiconductor*.

If you form a junction between n–type and p–type silicon, something wonderful happens. For complicated reasons, details of which we need not go into, electrons find it very easy to cross the junction from the n–type to the p–type silicon, but virtually impossible to go the other way. This is a *diode*, and it has the useful property of being able to conduct electricity in one direction, but not in the opposite one. The two terminals of the diode are called the *anode* (connected to the p–type material) and the *cathode* (connected to the n–type). When the anode is positive of the cathode, the diode behaves like a conductor, and current will flow. Otherwise, the diode behaves like a highly effective insulator. Fig 9 illustrates, in schematic form, the structure of a silicon diode.

A diode has a small forward voltage, typically 0.6v for silicon diodes. This is the minimum voltage that must be applied (in the forward direction) before conduction commences. Once the diode is conducting, this voltage remains effectively constant at 0.6v.

Diodes have two important ratings. One is the *maximum current* they can carry. If this is exceeded, the diode will overheat. The other is the *peak inverse voltage*, often abbreviated to piv. This is the (reverse) voltage at which the insulating property of the pn junction breaks down, and the diode will fall into conduction. Exceeding either of these two ratings is more than likely to destroy the diode.

There is one class of diode, useful in some situations, which is actually designed to break down safely. This is called the *zener diode*. At low values of reverse voltage, the zener diode functions as a normal diode – i.e. it refuses to conduct. At a certain voltage, however, it breaks down and starts to conduct. It now has the useful property that it will maintain this same voltage between its terminals *irrespective of the current through it*. In other words, unlike a resistor, it does not obey Ohm's law, which would predict that as current increased, the voltage would rise. Zener diodes are useful in voltage stabilisers and the like.

One further type of diode is the *light emitting diode*, or LED. This works like an ordinary diode – it conducts in the forward direction only. Electrons migrate from the n–type to the p–type region. Once there, some of them are captured by the atoms of impurity which are short of an electron. In being captured, the electrons lose energy, which they emit as visible light. By careful control of the exact levels of impurity manufacturers can control the colour of the light emitted. Red, green, yellow, orange and (more recently) blue LEDs can be obtained. They are much more durable than filament lamps, which work by heating a length of tungsten wire until it glows white hot. After a while, the tungsten wire will simply melt and the lamp will require replacement. LEDs, by contrast, work at 'cold'

temperatures and have virtually unlimited lifetimes.

An LED should always be used in conjunction with a resistor to limit its current. Unlike a bulb, which is connected directly across a 12v supply, the LED should be connected via a resistor, typically around 1k, to limit the current through it. Figure 8(c) shows how diodes, including zeners and LEDs are represented on circuit diagrams.

Transistors

The *transistor* is a three–terminal device, developed from the diode. Instead of two semiconductor layers, the p–type anode and n–type cathode of a diode, the transistor has three. In most transistors these are in the form of a 'sandwich', with an n–type *emitter* and another n–type layer called the *collector* forming the 'bread' of the sandwich, and a very thin p–type layer, called the *base* forming the sandwich 'filling'. For obvious reasons, this is called an *npn* transistor.

The base and emitter of the transistor work exactly like a diode. If the base is negative of the emitter, no current flows. The transistor is said to be 'off'. If the base voltage is raised to the +0.6v forward voltage that will enable the base–emitter diode to conduct, then current will start to flow from the base into the emitter. The transistor has now switched 'on'.

What makes the transistor incredibly useful is that the emitter and collector, in effect, form the ends of a resistor whose value is dependent on the base–to–emitter current. The resistance when no base current flows is extremely high (many megohms), but at even very small base currents, the effective resistance between emitter and collector drops to just a few ohms.

Why is this useful? The answer is that we can use it to control very large currents, several amps or more, by very small ones, perhaps just a milliamp or two. The transistor is a *current amplifier*, and we shall see its use in just such an application shortly. The current gain of a transistor is the ratio of its base to collector current.

To summarise, if the base of an npn transistor is 0.6v above its emitter, a small current flows from base to emitter, the transistor is switched 'on', and large currents can flow through the low effective resistance between collector and emitter. In normal operation, the collector will be held positive of the emitter, so current will flow from collector to emitter. If the base voltage falls below +0.6v, the transistor is 'off' and no current flows anywhere.

In a *pnp* transistor, the semiconductor 'sandwich' is reversed, the emitter and collector this time being of p–type material and the base being n–type. The principle of operation is exactly the same, but with all the voltages reversed. This time, the base must be at –0.6v with respect to the emitter before any current can flow, and the collector is now held negative of the emitter, so that the current will flow from emitter to collector. Fig 8(d) shows how npn and pnp transistors are represented on circuit diagrams.

Transistors have several ratings. One is the *maximum collector–emitter voltage*, V_{CE}. Normally this is quite a lot higher than the voltages we are likely to meet in our model railway, so it is usually irrelevant. Of more importance is the *maximum collector current*, I_C, and the *maximum total power*, P_{TOT}. Low-power transistors come in small plastic packages. They have a power rating well below one watt. High–power transistors are generally in metal cases, and can be mounted on finned aluminium heatsinks to help dissipate the large amount of heat they produce. A table in the Appendix gives the ratings of some transistors useful to railway modellers.

Integrated Circuits

Transistors and diodes are examples of *discrete semiconductor devices*. The plastic package in which they are supplied contains a single chip of silicon on which the n– and p–regions of the transistor or diode are formed and the package contains just one device. However, it is possible to form a great many transistors on the same chip of silicon, and thereby to make a

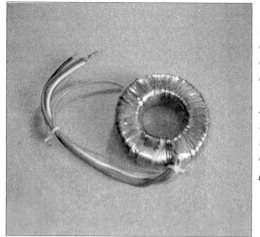

Toroidal transformers have a number of advantages in the model railway environment compared with the conventional chassis mounted type. The obvious one of these is reduced space and they are available in varying ratings and outputs. As with any transformers it essential they are securely mounted and the windings protected. (See right – underside of 'Whitchurch'.)

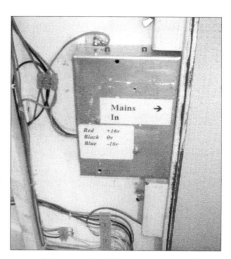

complete electronic circuit within a single package. This is called an *integrated circuit*, or IC. ICs vary in complexity from simple amplifiers and sensors up to whole computer processors containing millions of transistors all one the same small chip of silicon. We shall have occasion to meet one or two ICs later.

Electromagnetic devices

What we have discussed thus far falls under the general heading of *electronics*. This is concerned with the motion of tiny charged particles (electrons) through circuits. To do useful work on a model railway, however, we need to translate the motion of these tiny particles into large–scale actions, such as turning an electric motor to propel a train, throw a point or change a signal. In other words, we need a mechanical result from our electrical current. To obtain this, we use devices which generally employ *Electromagnetism* in one form or another.

Magnetism is a strange phenomenon. Indeed, it drove many of our pioneering physicists to distraction as they tried to understand it. We do not need the full theory to understand the electromagnetic devices we use in model railways. However, understanding how they work is easier with a little bit of an idea of what is going on, so we can simplify the most important principles as follows:

A *magnetic field* is set up by a *moving* electrical charge (i.e. an electric current). This is the principle behind solenoids and relays.

A *stationary* charge (e.g. an electron) in a constant magnetic field experiences no *magnetic force*. However, if the charge *moves* within the field (e.g. as part of an electric current flow), then it experiences such a force. This phenomenon is used in electric motors.

If, instead of moving a charge within the magnetic field, we arrange for the magnetic field to *change*, then even a stationary charge will experience a *magnetic force*, thereby moving it (and thus setting up an electric current). This principle is used in transformers.

Solenoids

From our first principle, above, a magnetic field is set up whenever a current flows. A highly efficient way to produce this magnetic field is to arrange a length of conductor (eg copper wire) in the form of a tightly wrapped coil and to pass a large current through it. The magnetic field will be directed along the centre of the coil. What we have is an *electromagnet*. When current flows through the wire, a magnetic field is produced. When the current ceases, the field disappears.

Certain substances (iron is a good one) are highly susceptible to magnetic fields. In a *solenoid*, an iron plunger, concentric with the coil, is free to move to and fro along the axis of the coil. In one type of solenoid, the plunger is normally held by a spring a little way out of the coil. When current flows through the coil, the magnetic field so produced pulls the plunger into the coil against the force of the spring. When current is switched off, the spring forces the plunger back into its starting position. This type of solenoid is best suited to applications where most of the time the coil is unenergised, since otherwise there would be a continuous current drain on the power supply. One example might be operating signals, especially in situations where the signal spent most of its time at 'danger'. The mechanical linkage between solenoid and signal would be arranged so that the 'danger' setting corresponded to the *unenergised* position of the solenoid.

A second type of solenoid employs two separate coils, and a plunger which is able to move between them. When current is passed through the left–hand coil, the plunger moves left. When current passes through the right–hand coil, the plunger moves right. A latching mechanism ensures that the plunger remains in position after the current is turned off. This type of solenoid only needs current when the plunger is to be moved, and is suited to applications such as operating points. A relatively large effort, and consequently a high current, is needed to change a point. However, once the point setting is changed, with this type of solenoid the current can be switched off, and the solenoid need draw no further current until we need to change it again.

Relays

Relays are based on exactly the same principle as solenoids, except that we now have, instead of a plunger to operate external mechanical devices, an internal actuator which opens or closes one or more pairs of switch contacts.

As with the solenoid, there will be two connections for the operating coil, plus another set of connections for the switch contacts. In the simplest case there will be three of these. The first will be connected to a contact which is moved by the actuator when the relay is energised. The other two will be connected to fixed contacts, one of them (the *normally closed* contact, NC) is placed so that the moving contact touches it when the relay is unenergised, and the other (the *normally open* contact, NO) is placed so that the moving contact touches it when the relay is energised. This is called the *Single Pole Changeover* relay, SPCO for short. In a *Double Pole Changeover* (DPCO) relay, there are two switched contacts, each with its own NO and NC contacts. Three and four–pole relays can be obtained.

The utility of the relay lies in its ability to allow one circuit (that of the energising coil) to control one or more other circuits (via the switch contacts) without any electrical connection between them. The occasions on which we find this useful are legion, as will become apparent later on.

The important parameters of a relay are its operating voltage and coil resistance. The latter might be around 400 ohms for a miniature relay with an operating voltage of 12v.

Motors

Electric motors work on the second of our 'principles of magnetism', which says that a moving charge, within a magnetic field, experiences a magnetic force. The moving charge in a motor is the current through a coil called the winding, the magnetic field is provided by a permanent magnet, and the consequent force is used to spin the winding around in the magnet's field.

In operating points, motors are generally used to rotate a captive nut, which propels a threaded rod to provide the point movement. At each end of its travel, the rod operates a switch mechanism which cuts out the supply to the motor in that direction. Using diodes, however, we can ensure that the motor is still able to travel in the other direction until it meets the corresponding end stop there (see chapter 4, fig 19). This type of point motor is generally wired so that one terminal is held at zero volts, and the other at a positive or negative voltage. Positive will send the motor one way, and negative the other.

Transformers

Our third principle of magnetism referred to the fact that when a magnetic field changes, a stationary charged particle will experience a magnetic force. If the particle is an electron inside a good conductor, this force will propel it, and its neighbours, along the conductor, thus setting up an *electric current*. This is the principle used in the *transformer*.

A transformer has two coils, called the primary and secondary windings, wound around a common core. Into the primary we feed an *alternating current*, generally from the ac mains. This current will set up a magnetic field which passes through the centre of the primary winding. Because the windings are concentric, this same magnetic field also passes through the secondary.

Now, if the magnetic field produced by the primary winding were constant there would be no effect on the secondary. Electrons in the conductor forming the secondary winding would be unaffected by the field since, although they are charged particles, they are stationary and thus do not feel a magnetic field (this is our second principle, above). Hence, a transformer cannot operate on *direct current* (dc).

However, because the primary is fed from a source of alternating current the field through the windings is not constant. It is varying very rapidly, changing direction 50 times a second. This means that the electrons in the secondary winding do feel a magnetic force, and its effect is to push them, first one way, then the other through the secondary winding. If we connected the secondary up to an external circuit, we would find that an alternating voltage would appear across the secondary winding, and could be used to drive electrons round the circuit.

The strength of the magnetic field produced by a coil depends on (a) the number of turns and (b) the current through the coil. Thus if the primary has a large number of turns, it will produce a strong field. On the secondary side, the magnitude of the induced alternating voltage depends on the strength of the field produced by the primary and the number of turns in the secondary coil. The strength of the primary field, however, is determined by the number of turns on the primary winding, so we find that the ratio of the secondary voltage to the primary voltage is exactly the same as the ratio between their respective number of turns.

The transformer is therefore able to take one ac voltage (say 240v ac mains) and change (or transform) it into another, say 15v ac. Some transformers might have more than one secondary winding, in which case they can be used completely independently, or wired in series to give a higher secondary voltage.

Transformers are rated according to their *maximum total power*. For reasons that need not concern us here, power in ac devices such as transformers is quoted in VA (standing for volt–amps) rather than watts. Thus a 30VA transformer might have two 15v ac windings. These could be used as two separate 15v supplies, with 1A available in each. Or, they could be wired in series to give a single 30v, again at 1A maximum current. Or finally, the two 15v windings could be used in parallel, to provide 15v at 2A current. The essential thing is that the total 30VA should not be exceeded.

Chapter 3

POWER SUPPLIES and CONTROLLERS

In this chapter, we shall develop the circuit for a simple fixed voltage power supply, with which solenoids, relays, point motors and the lights on station buildings can be driven. We then go on to discuss an electronic controller for the model railway.

Before embarking on this subject, we should perhaps start off with a safety notice. It is *absolutely essential* that all exposed mains terminals, for example the primary winding tags on a transformer, are kept well out of reach. Preferably, they should be totally enclosed inside a metal container (e.g. an aluminium box) which is securely earthed. On no account should you rely on insulating tape wrapped around the transformer to provide the protection. Tape loses its stickiness over time, and the terminals may become exposed with possibly fatal results. The best way to connect your transformer on the mains side is to use an IEC Euro style mains chassis plug and a matching Euro style line socket (like the one on an electric kettle). The chassis plug fits into a rectangular hole in your aluminium box, and the transformer's 240v winding tags are wired directly to the live and neutral,

the earth being securely connected to the metal box.

At the other end of the cable you should ensure that your mains plug is fitted with a suitable fuse. A 13A fuse is completely out of order. The use of a 13A fuse on the primary side of the transformer would provide next to no protection whatsoever on the secondary side. In a transformer of good efficiency, the ratio of primary to secondary current is roughly in the inverse ratio of primary to secondary voltage. Most of what we use on the model railway will come out of a 12v secondary, so the primary current will be approximately twenty times less than the secondary current. Thus a 13A fuse on the primary side will blow when 260A is drawn from the secondary. Needless to say, most of the circuitry will be well cooked long before this! A 1A fuse in your mains plug will provide somewhat more sensible protection.

If you are at all unsure about constructing your own mains–connected equipment, then by all means purchase suitable power units from commercial sources. Suitable transformer/rectifier units can be obtained from a variety of suppliers, and provided they have the right voltage and an adequate

current rating for the task to hand, they will work perfectly well with the other circuits mentioned in this book.

A 12 volt fixed supply

The circuit shown in fig 10 is for a fixed 12v supply, which provides a maximum current of 1A. The primary side of the transformer is wired to the 240v ac mains. The secondary winding delivers 12v ac. If the supply is to provide a maximum current of 1A, the transformer should have a power rating of at least 12VA. In fact, it is always a good idea to use a transformer with a little more power in reserve, so a 15VA or 20VA transformer would be ideal.

We have shown the mains earth lead connected to the metal chassis or box in which the mains transformer should be screened. However, the connection from earth to the negative output from the supply is shown only as a dotted line. Care must be taken when connecting the earth to the output side, especially when multiple supplies/controllers are used. There is the possibility of short circuits through such earth connections. We shall refer to this point again later.

The transformer feeds what looks like four separate diodes arranged in a diamond

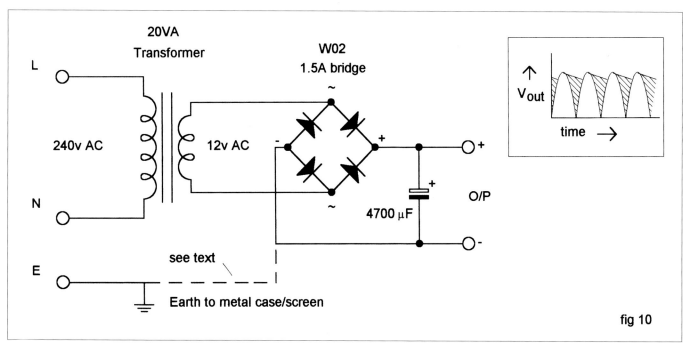

fig 10

21

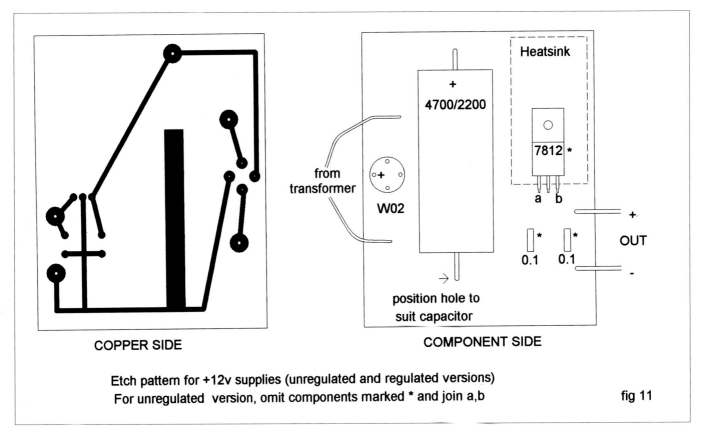

COPPER SIDE   COMPONENT SIDE

Etch pattern for +12v supplies (unregulated and regulated versions)
For unregulated version, omit components marked * and join a,b   fig 11

formation. These diodes form a *bridge rectifier*. You could use four discrete diodes and connect them up as shown, but this arrangement is so commonly used that component manufacturers provide the four diodes conveniently connected up in a single bridge rectifier package.

Recall that our transformer operates only on ac. Its secondary winding will provide a continuously varying voltage with either end of the secondary winding flipping polarity fifty times a second. However, most applications on model railways require dc rather than ac. The purpose of the rectifier is to ensure that, on each half–cycle of voltage we supply our 'positive' terminal from whichever end of the transformer secondary winding is positive, and we supply the 'negative' terminal from whichever end is negative. If you follow a path through the diodes, you will see that this is the case.

The purpose of the capacitor in fig 10 is to 'smooth' the output voltage. The rectifier ensures that the output voltage is

always of the same polarity, i.e. that it is dc, but the instantaneous value of the voltage will still vary. In effect, we have taken the 'negative' half–cycles of the ac voltage and connected them to the output terminals the other way round, thus effectively converting them to positive half–cycles. However, the voltage will still drop down to zero and back up again twice every cycle.

Remember that the capacitor can store charge. What happens is that when the voltage at the rectifier '+' output is approaching maximum, the capacitor takes in a proportion of the output current and stores it as a charge on its plates. When the rectifier voltage falls, the charge in the capacitor cannot find its way back through the diodes (check the direction in which the diodes conduct). Therefore, the capacitor discharges out via the supply terminals. Its voltage will drop as it discharges, but if its capacitance is large enough then the voltage drop can be kept small.

Suppose we decided that a drop of 2 volts between half–cycles was acceptable. We would require a capacitor that could supply 1A of discharge current for one hundredth of a second and in doing so drop no more than 2v. Using the equation $Q = It$ from the last chapter, we see that the charge (Q) represented by one amp (I) flowing for 0.01 sec (t) is 0.01 coulomb. Using the equation $Q = CV$, and specifying V (the voltage change when the capacitor loses 0.01 coulomb of charge) as 2v, we see that $C = 0.005$ farad, or 4,700µf (the nearest standard value). In the small inset diagram the clear curves represent the 'raw' rectified output from the bridge rectifier and the hatched areas represent the time during which the capacitor discharges. The actual output voltage thus resembles a saw–tooth wave.

As it stands, the circuit will meet our requirement to supply 12v at 1A, but it is far from ideal. Its first disadvantage is that there is no built–in *protection* against a short circuit. If the output terminals are inadvertently shorted together, then very much more than 1A will flow. This will either destroy the rectifier, burnt out the transformer, or both. Secondly, the circuit has a relatively large *ripple voltage*. We have seen that its output will ripple by 2v or so every hundredth of a second. The ripple could be made smaller by using a larger capacitance, but such capacitors are bulky and very expensive. Thirdly, the circuit has poor *regulation*. The transformer will be designed to supply a nominal 12v ac output, but its actual output voltage will be considerably more than this at low output current and will reduce as the output current increases. The reason for this is that the windings themselves have a finite resistance, and although this might only be a few ohms, at 1A current, this will correspond to the loss of several volts. Thus our nominal 12v supply might well produce 15v at low loads and 10v at full load.

An Improved Circuit

The circuit in fig 12 overcomes these problems by using an integrated circuit *voltage regulator*. In effect, this uses an electronic circuit to sense the difference between the supply voltage and the desired output voltage, and to subtract exactly this amount from the supply voltage to provide the output voltage. The voltage regulator IC has three terminals, an input, an output and a common. The smoothing capacitor is connected between the IC input and common, and the output terminals are connected to the IC output and common.

Notice that we have used a 15v transformer this time, but a rather smaller smoothing capacitor. The reason for this is that the regulator IC needs an input voltage that never drops below the desired output voltage (12v). However, it will not be upset by quite large amounts of ripple voltage, so we can use a smaller capacitor. The two 0.1μF capacitors are to prevent instability in the regulator.

The regulator will produce quite a lot of heat. At 1A, it might be required to drop from 15v input to 12v output, so the voltage across it will be 3v, meaning 3W of power will go into producing heat. The device should therefore be mounted on a heatsink.

The circuit shown uses a type 7812 regulator. This provides +12v at 1A with a typical regulation of 0.2%, that is, the output voltage will vary by less than 0.2% between no load and full load. This is obviously a vast improvement on our earlier circuit. The 78 series of regulators also have built–in overload protection so that accidental short–circuits will not harm them.

A Dual Polarity Supply

Fig 13 shows a further development of the +12v regulated supply, this time providing –12v also. This will be useful if you wish to operate points or signals using a bi–directional motor.

Note that we have now used a 50VA transformer with two 15v secondary windings. These are joined in series (the transformer instructions should indicate which end of the windings to connect) and the bridge rectifier should now be rated at 100 piv. The rectifier this time feeds two smoothing capacitors. These are connected in series, with their junction wired to the transformer secondary junction, as shown. Take *immense care* over polarity. If you get this wrong, the capacitors will be destroyed at the moment of switching on.

The positive terminal of the bridge rectifier, as before, feeds the positive terminal of one capacitor. The other capacitor is wired with its positive terminal

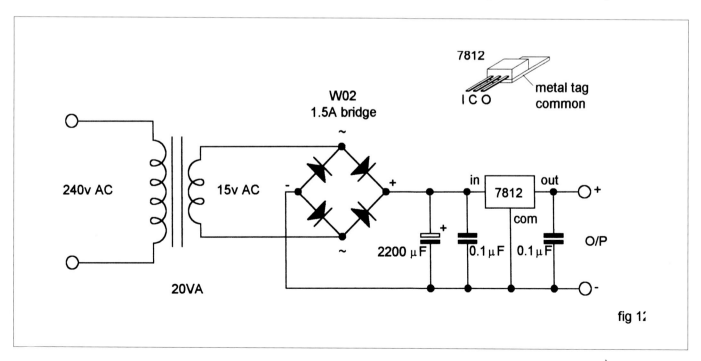

fig 1:

connected to 0v, and its negative terminal is fed by the negative output of the bridge rectifier. The +12v output is obtained from a 7812 regulator, as before. The −12v output is obtained from a 7912 negative voltage regulator. This is exactly like a 7812, except that the input and output voltages are negative of the common, rather than positive as in the 7812. You should be careful to note the different pin configuration.

Other regulators are available for different voltages and currents. The 78xx series are positive voltage regulators with maximum current of 1A. The 'xx' denotes the output voltage, thus 7806, 7808, 7812, 7815 etc. The 79xx regulators are similar, but provide negative voltage outputs. The 78Sxx provide 2A output current and the 78Txx provide 3A.

Circuit Construction

This might be an opportune time for a few words on construction methods. How do we translate the circuit diagram into a physical piece of hardware that we can incorporate into the layout?

We first reiterate the safety message. A secure earth, good insulation of the transformer primary, a proper mains cable connection and a sensible fuse are the essentials.

You may wish to use a toroidal transformer. These are shaped like doughnuts, unlike the usual box–shaped transformers; this makes them very suitable for placing under the baseboard. If you use a toroidal transformer, be aware that they tend to have very high current surge at switch–on. Therefore, you should protect these with an anti–surge fuse.

Once you are past the mains transformer, provided you have a secure earth connection, safety is not so much of an issue. You can still destroy expensive electronic components, but people are generally safe! The main issue here is reliability. I have seen layouts where under the baseboard, diodes, relays, resistors etc are soldered directly to each other, without any structural support, the whole thing resembling a rather badly built bird's nest. This is not just untidy, it is prone to short–circuits, broken wires, and all kinds of other problems which will make it a nightmare to maintain.

Electronic components should be securely mounted so that they are properly supported and cannot flop around. There are several ways of doing this. The first is to mount them on a tag board. This is a rectangle of SRBP board (a good insulator) with two rows of solder tags along the two long sides. Each solder tag has two holes: one in which the component is placed and another for any connecting wire(s). The tags are pre–tinned to make soldering easy, and a row of central 6BA clearance holes makes mounting the tag board straightforward. Tag boards are suitable for resistors, capacitors, diodes etc but they are NOT suitable for components requiring heat sinks. For the latter, it is essential that the heat sink is securely bolted to a firm mounting surface.

The second approach is to use stripboard. This is SRBP board with a matrix of holes punched at 0.1" intervals, and copper strips on one side. Components are mounted on the non–copper side with their leads fed through the holes and soldered to the copper strip before clipping them to length. The required circuit connections are made by scraping away the copper strip, using a special spot–face cutter (or a large–size drill), and by linking strips where necessary with jumper wires. This approach can yield good results, although the large number of holes at relatively close intervals renders the

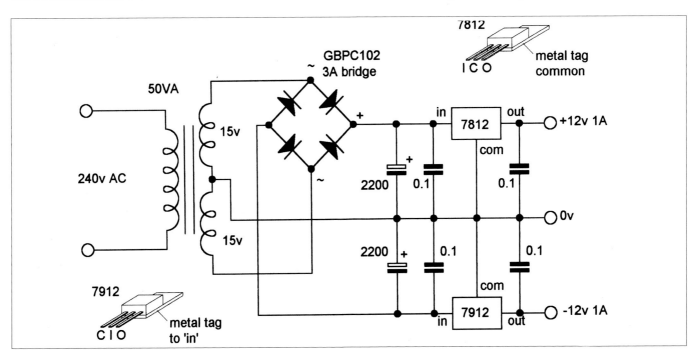

stripboard somewhat weak. If particularly heavy components, e.g. large relays, were mounted on it, there would be a danger of the board splitting.

A third alternative is to etch your own fibre glass printed circuit board, or pcb. This is not as difficult as you might think. The circuit connections are drawn out on the copper surface using a special etch–resist pen, or alternatively to get a rather neater job, you can purchase sheets of transfers to give you round pads, and flexible adhesive tape to join them. Once you have prepared the pattern on the copper surface, the board is immersed in a solution of ferric chloride for a few minutes. When it is taken out, all the copper will have been etched away, apart from where the etch–resist pen has drawn the required pattern, or where the transfers have protected the copper. The board is then rinsed under the tap, and the etch–resist pen or transfers removed using fine grade sandpaper. Holes are then drilled for components, which are mounted in a

similar way as on stripboard. This approach has the advantage that only the required holes are drilled, and fibre glass is intrinsically a lot stronger than SRBP board. Therefore, you can mount relatively heavy components on a fibre glass pcb without problems.

A further refinement is to use pcb which can be purchased ready coated with a photosensitive etch resist material. When this is exposed to ultra violet light (UV lamp or strong sunlight), it breaks down and can be rinsed away with a dilute (7%) caustic soda solution. The etch pattern can be either printed or photocopied onto overhead transparency film, which is used as a template, placed over the photosensitive copper–clad board and exposed to UV. Where the pattern is black, no UV penetrates and the photosensitive etch resist is intact. Where the pattern is clear, the UV breaks down the etch resist. After rinsing with dilute caustic soda and thoroughly rinsing under the tap, the board can be etched in the normal way with ferric

chloride. However, unlike the method using tape and transfers, we have not destroyed our template, which can then be re–used to make further identical boards. There are a number of circuits, such as relay and solenoid drivers which you may need many times on your layout. It is useful to be able to mass–produce them in this way. Etch patterns for the circuits in this book are given in figures 11, 14 and 16.

A Train Controller

In controlling a train, we require a continuously variable power supply, that goes down to zero volts, and can be smoothly increased to maximum. Unfortunately, there is no IC that fulfils these requirements. There are ICs that will allow variable output voltages, but none (so far as I am aware) that will actually go down to zero volts. Even a volt or two is liable to cause an engine to 'creep'.

Therefore, fig 15 shows a suitable

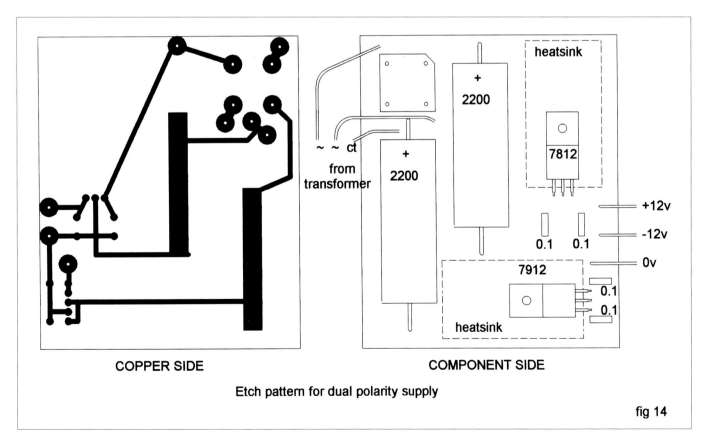

COPPER SIDE   COMPONENT SIDE

Etch pattern for dual polarity supply

fig 14

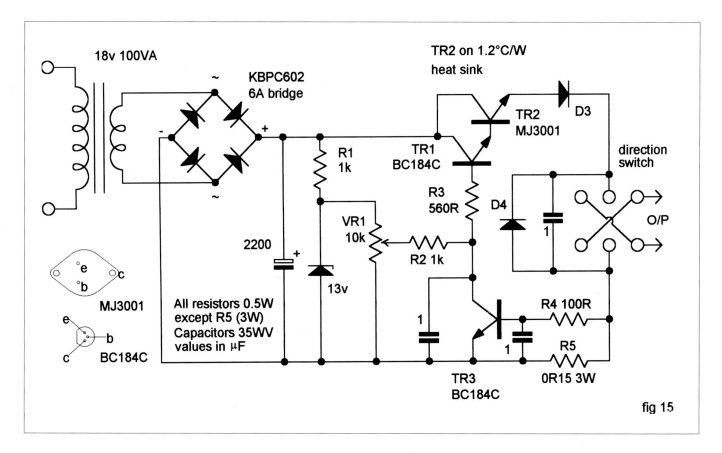

fig 15

circuit built out of discrete components. I have built quite a number of controllers with this same basic circuit over the last twenty years, and it has proved an extremely reliable 'no frills' controller.

The circuit is fed by the usual transformer/rectifier/smoothing capacitor combination. Note that this time, we use an 18v 100VA transformer and a 6A rectifier. This is suitable for large '0' gauge engines drawing up to four amps. If you do not need this much current, then both the VA rating of the transformer and the current rating of the rectifier can be reduced accordingly. As mentioned earlier, if you prefer, you can purchase a ready–made 16–18v supply of suitable current rating and use this with the rest of this circuit.

Immediately after the smoothing capacitor, a 1k resistor feeds a 13v zener diode. Remember that a zener diode, connected in reverse, will maintain its breakdown voltage irrespective of the current through it. Thus, the voltage across

the potentiometer remains 13v, irrespective of any fluctuations in the power supply voltage caused by increasing load, etc. If you want a slightly higher maximum output voltage, use a 15v or 16v diode instead.

From the potentiometer slider, we draw off a voltage which can be varied smoothly from zero to +13v. This voltage feeds current via resistors R2 and R3 into the base of transistor TR1. Now remember that the transistor is a current amplifier. The base current, in this case a fraction of a milliamp, is multiplied by the transistor's current gain to give a collector to emitter current of a few mA. This is then fed into the base of TR2, which is an MJ3001 power transistor which has a very high current gain of 1,000. The MJ3001 can multiply this current up to several amps if necessary. This is then fed to the positive output terminal via diode D3. The voltage at the positive output terminal rises, until it gets to a point where it is equal to to the voltage at the potentiometer slider, less the

two forward voltages at the base–emitter junctions of TR1 and TR2. At this point, TR1 and TR2 will just be in conduction. If the output voltage rose any more, then they would start to turn off, thus reducing the output current and thereby causing the output voltage to fall again. The output current will automatically adjust itself so that the output voltage is held fixed a little below the voltage on the slider of VR1. As the voltage at VR1 is changed, so the output voltage changes accordingly. We have, in effect, a voltage regulator whose voltage can be adjusted using VR1 to any value we require.

Note that diodes D3 and D4 are protection diodes designed to prevent the circuit being damaged by any external voltage which may be fed into the controller. They are not absolutely necessary, and may be dispensed with, particularly if you only have one controller on the layout. If fitted, note that D3 must be rated to carry the maximum output current.

All too often a railway which has taken countless hours – and £'s to built or collect can be ruined through poor control and running. 'Ferring' owned and operated by Michael Ball of the Epson & Ewell Club runs as well as it looks. A credit to the care taken in planning, construction and building.

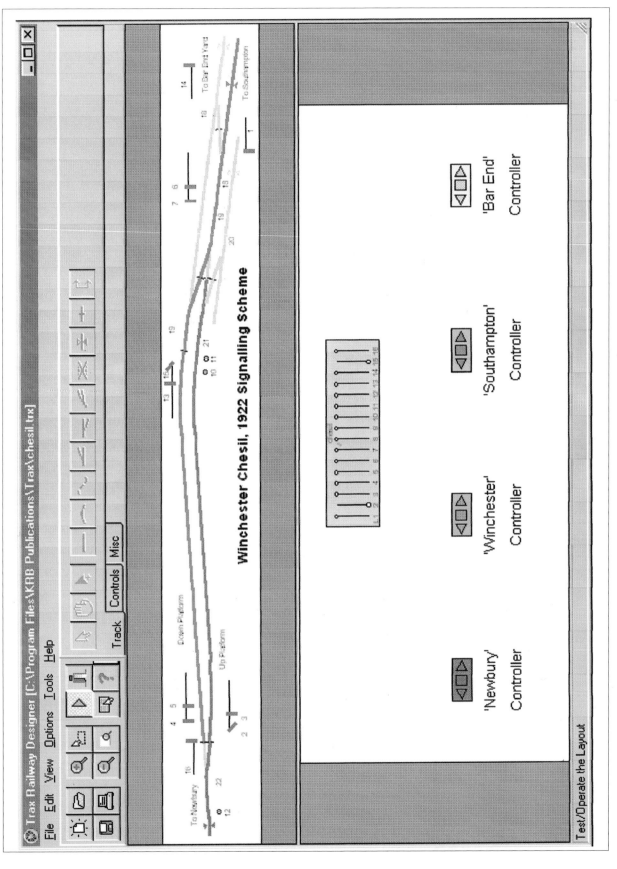

Screen shot of the 'CHESIL.TRX' sample file as included in the programme. (To produce this image on your computer, firstly open the TRAX programme. Then click FILE then OPEN. Select CHESIL.TRX and then the TEST/OPERATE button. – see key on opposite page. In the illustration, levers 2 and 15 have been reversed.) Note in actual practice signals 6/7 and 14 were further south than shown but they are included in their present position to allow the complete image to be easily reproduced on the screen.

28

Right; Also included in the sample files within the TRAX programme is Whitchurch3.Trx. Again depicted in the TEST/ OPERATE mode and with levers 3, 4 , 7 and 8 reversed on the red controller.

If you find when viewing this image the signals appear only as red lines, increase the size of the image until the full display is provided.

Lower; Regardless of which toolbar you are working with, Track / Controls / Misc, the 'Hand – Move Tool, is common as is the 'Arrow' used for select.

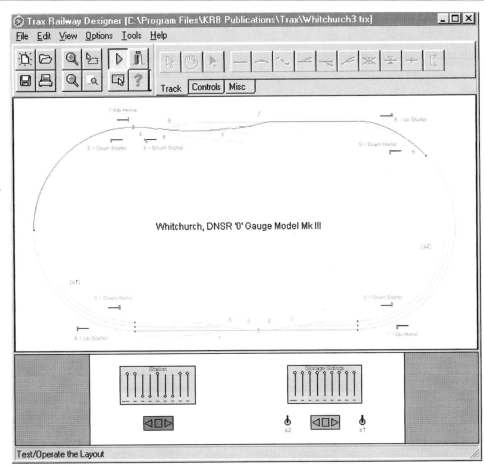

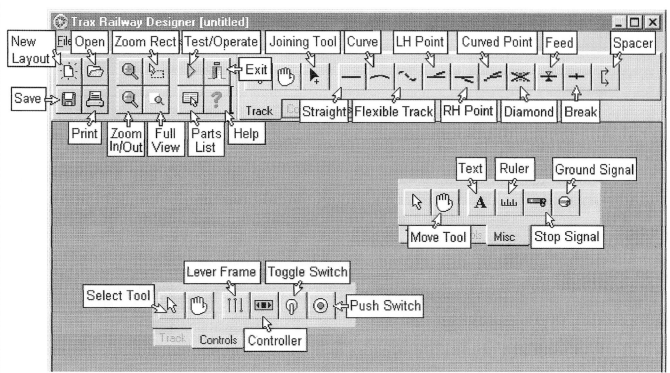

'Aveton Gifford' from the fiddle yard and viewed towards the station. The goods train has been accepted by the controller and by pulling off the appropriate lever, the 'disc' signal has come 'off' and the train can proceed with power applied to the section ahead. Note that as with prototype practice it is essential not to restore the signal lever until the complete train has passed all the points locked by that signal. In model terms the result could also be a 'rough–shunt' as the power to the track were suddenly removed. The semaphore arms could also do with being a bit more horizontal in their 'on' positions.

This is the view not normally seen by the public or the operators and does show up where items still need to be finished – is any railway ever really finished?

We come now to the circuitry around TR3. This is basically an overload protection circuit, which is designed to prevent excessive current being drawn in the event of a short–circuit. The critical thing to remember is that a transistor is off if it doesn't have the minimum 0.6v at its base–emitter junction. In normal operation of the controller, TR3 is off and takes no part in the circuit operation. Notice that the load current returns to the controller at the negative output terminal and thence via resistor R5 back to the rectifier. The resistor R5 is used as a current–sensing device, and its value, 0R15, is critical. By Ohm's law, if the output current is 4A, the voltage across R5 will rise to 4 x 0.15 = 0.6v. Below 4A of output current, the voltage across R5 will be less than this and TR3 remains turned off. However, because the emitter and base of TR3 are connected across R5, when the voltage across R5 reaches 0.6v (i.e. the output current is 4A) TR3 will start to turn on, drawing collector current from

the potentiometer slider via R2. This will rob TR1 of some of its base current, thereby reducing the current drive to TR2, and limiting any further increase in output current. Thus, the output of the controller is limited to 4A, even in the case of a dead short.

Of course, if you do not need 4A, it is a needless waste of money to use a 100VA transformer and 6A rectifier. You could reduce these to, say, 50VA and 3A, and double the value of R5 to 0R3. Doubling the value of R5 means that it would reach the critical 0.6v at only half the output current, i.e. the output would be limited to 2A instead of 4. If you used exclusively the very low current coreless motors, you could restrict the maximum current to 100mA, say, by using a value of 60R for R5. Current can be limited to any desired value – simply use Ohm's law to find the value of R5 that would give 0.6v at the desired limiting current. A further refinement we have used in the Winchester Test Track controllers is to use two 0R3

resistors in parallel, one of which can be switched out of the circuit, thus allowing us to set the maximum current to either 2A or 4A.

If you do need the full output, you should mount TR2 on a heatsink of 1.2°C/W. Heatsinks are rated in terms of *degrees celsius per watt*. This means, that for every 1 watt of power dissipated in the transistor or IC the heatsink will radiate enough heat to limit the temperature rise to 1.2°C. You should try to limit temperature rises to below 100°C. In the case of a dead short, the MJ3001 will be passing a current of up to 4A, with a collector voltage around 18v, so the power dissipated will be 72W. A 1.2°C/W heatsink should cope with this. If you do not need 4A, but say only 2A, then a heatsink of 2.4°C/W should suffice.

Returning briefly to the topic of earth connection: do not earth the negative side of the smoothing capacitor, as is conventional with fixed supplies (see fig

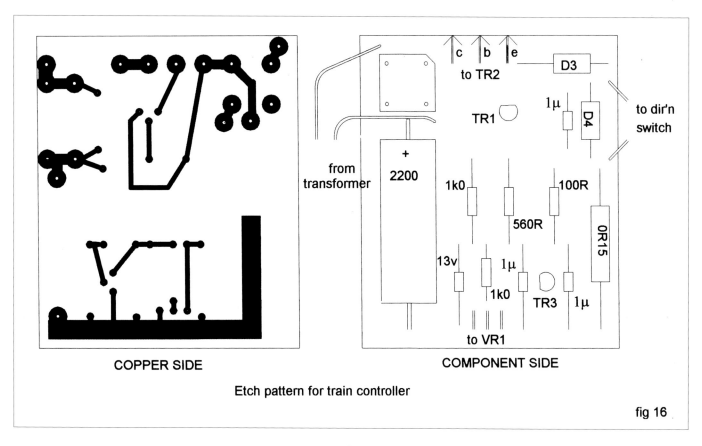

COPPER SIDE   COMPONENT SIDE

Etch pattern for train controller

fig 16

11). Earth connection must be made *after* the direction switch. The reason for this is two–fold. Firstly, if the switch were faulty, the earth connection would no longer be effective. Secondly, if something on the track side were earthed then this would short out the current–sensing resistor R5 and overload protection would be ineffective.

Meters

Ideally, your controllers should have both a voltmeter connected across the output (connected between anode and cathode of D4) and an ammeter in series with it (connected between the cathode of D3 and the input to the direction switch). Unless you use a centre–zero meter, you cannot put the ammeter after the direction switch, as polarity can be reversed.

The presence of both of these will make fault diagnosis easy, and you can often spot problems before they become too severe. The voltmeter will basically tell you whether the controller is working correctly, i.e. does it rise smoothly as the potentiometer is wound up. The presence of any jerkiness or flat spots when there is no external load will indicate a fault in the controller. If the voltage is correct, the ammeter will enable you to diagnose faults in your locomotives and track wiring. No current but a reasonable voltage reading indicates a pick–up or wiring fault, a large current and a voltage which drops to zero indicates a short–circuit. A current which fluctuates indicates a locomotive with a 'sticky' point in its motion, most generally associated with badly quartered wheels or coupling rods too tight. You will get to know how much current your locos normally take, so if you find one taking a lot more, it probably needs a little lubrication.

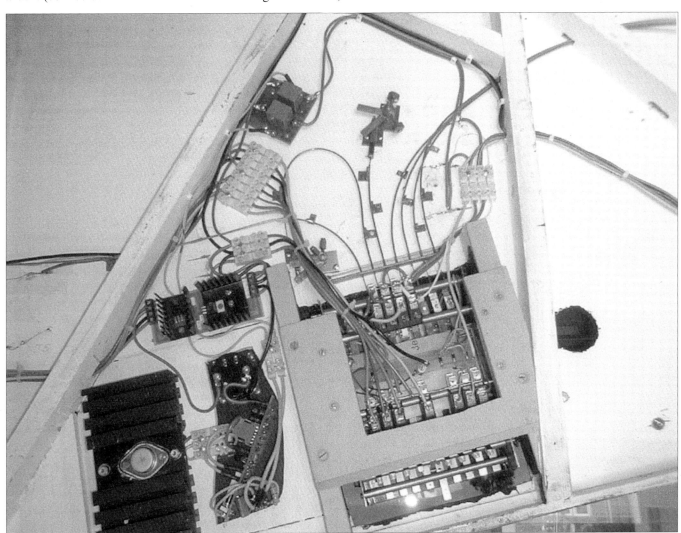

The underside of my own Whitchurch layout and included to show the lever frame, hopefully neat wiring – it makes life a lot easier if something goes wrong, and various components described in the text. Notice the all important heat sinks.

OPERATING POINTS and SIGNALS

In this chapter, we shall consider the various methods available for operating points and signals on the layout. Again, we shall introduce one or two electronic circuits, using the basic components introduced earlier.

There are three aspects to operating points. Firstly, we need to mechanically move the blades of the switch from left to right. Secondly, we need to ensure that the crossing vee is fed from the correct terminal of the controller. In other words, it must be connected to one or other of the stock rails, depending on the point setting. Thirdly, in some cases, we may need a control voltage which will switch from one (fixed) value to another when the point setting changes. This control voltage might, for example, determine whether a track break is bridged or not (see fig 6, for example). In the case of signals, the first and third of these aspects apply equally. The second, of course, does not.

Manual Operation

The simplest method of operating points and signals is by hand. We simply move the point switch, or the signal operating lever with our finger. Although simple and straightforward, this is generally felt to be less than satisfactory by most modellers. For one thing, the appearance of a giant hand somewhat detracts from the illusion of a world in miniature, and for another, the point or signal in question may be difficult to reach.

An improvement on the finger scheme is the wire–in–tube method. Here, 0.025" piano wire is fed through 1/16" brass tube. At one end, the wires can be attached to a realistic lever–frame as in a full size signal box. You can either make your own, or purchase one of several kits of parts on the market.

The tube must be held firmly in place, for example by feeding it through holes in brackets made of brass angle. If the tube is soldered to the brackets, and the brackets are securely screwed to the underside of the base board, then you will find that when one end of the wire is moved, the motion is faithfully reproduced at the other end. If the tube is able to move, or the brackets are so far apart that it can bend, then operation will be less than perfect.

This motion can be used to move the tie–bar of a set of points, or to move the operating lever of a signal by means of suitable cranks. Although it is very 'low–tech', I find the wire–in–tube method very satisfying. There is a pleasant tactile sensation in actually moving the points via a mechanical linkage, and, of course, it is the way things work in full–size practice.

The illustration on the opposite page illustrates the lever frame and the under–the–baseboard view of my own 0–gauge layout. Fortunately, most of the points are in and around the goods yard area, which is all on one baseboard. Thus with the lever frame on this baseboard, the wire–in–tube method can be used for a good proportion of the points and signals.

To operate signals, I use a sliding square brass bar with a ramp filed on one end. This operates against a spring loaded plunger and forces the signal operating wire up when the lever is pulled. In the case of points, to ensure fully adjustable operation, I have used two separately adjustable cranks, one for the left– and one for the right–hand setting.

It is essential, if using this scheme, that the lever frame should have some mechanism for locking the levers in both the normal and the reverse position, otherwise, the switch blades of the points will tend to creep open, with consequent derailment problems. The lever frame can

The Southampton Group of the Scalefour Society produced a 4mm model of Winchester Chesil rightly regarded as one of the finest and most accurate model representations ever built. It is now on permanent display at Milestones Museum in Basingstoke and where the principals of the original prototype route setting are used to feed power to the tracks as necessary. This is the view looking 'north towards Kings Worthy' and the 'fiddle yard'. Not surprisingly the signals themselves are the work of Peter Squibb – and the finials also have the correct slots in them!

also be equipped with microswitches, operated by the same lever mechanism as moves the wire. In some cases, you may find you need more than one microswitch on a given lever. One will switch the controller feed to the crossing vee, the other may be required to supply a control voltage, as discussed above.

The major drawback of the wire–in–tube method is that it is effectively restricted to situations where the operating levers and the points in question are on the same baseboard (in the case of portable layouts), and in any case, drives of any great length are impractical. Thus, for many situations, we are forced to use electromechanical methods of operation.

Solenoid Operation

A solenoid, as we have seen, involves feeding a large current through a coil. This sets up a magnetic field which in turn attracts a steel or iron plunger. The plunger operates a mechanical linkage to the point

blades or the signal arm. In one type of solenoid, a return spring pushes the plunger back when the current ceases. In another, a similar large current is fed through the second coil which pulls the plunger back in the other direction.

The type of solenoid which uses a return spring suffers from the drawback that current must be supplied for the whole of the time during which the point or signal is reversed. As soon as current ceases, it will return to its normal position under the action of the return spring. This is fine if the solenoid is one which takes only a small current, which in turn implies a relatively light load, such as a signal arm. To drive a set of points reliably, ample mechanical force must be available and this will require a large current. At any one time, there may be quite a number of points in the reverse position, so the power supply requirements would be considerable.

The second type of solenoid, where a second coil must be energised to return the

point or signal to normal, does not suffer from this drawback. Power is only applied whilst the plunger moves from one position to the other. In between times, no power is required. The solenoid coils could be operated directly from a power supply. It would simply be necessary to have a switch connecting the supply to each of the solenoid coils. The switch would need to be of a momentary type, such as a push–to–make button switch. However, such an arrangement would suffer from a number of disadvantages. Firstly, since the solenoid will require, let us say, 5 Amps to operate reliably, the power supply would need to be capable of providing this level of current. Such a supply would be very expensive. Secondly, if the push switch were held closed too long, or if it stuck in the closed position, there is every chance of burning out the coil. The resistance of these coils is very low – around three ohms is typical. Therefore, the power in the coil, whilst 5 Amps flows through it is quite large. Using

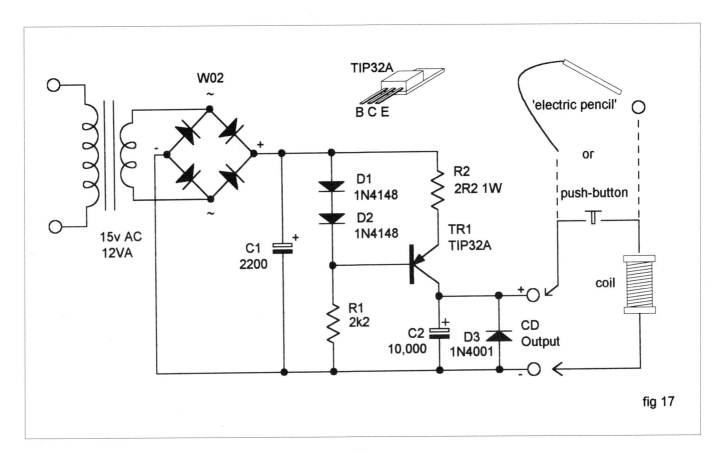

fig 17

the formula $P = I^2R$ we can see that it is (5 amps) times (5 amps) times (3 ohms) or 75 watts. Such power would produce a great deal of heat and soon melt our coil.

A Simple Capacitor Discharge Circuit

The circuit in fig 17 solves both of these problems. It is known as a capacitor discharge (CD) circuit, and it enables us to operate a 5 amp solenoid from a power supply which needs to produce no more than a fraction of an amp, and it prevents the solenoid coil from over–heating if the circuit is inadvertently left on too long. Let us consider how it works.

A 15v transformer is used, but it is unnecessary in this case to have an IC regulator. Current limiting is built into the CD circuit, and it is tolerant of a poorly regulated supply voltage. In this case, as current is very low, the 15v transformer will actually give us 18v or more at the smoothing capacitor. When the supply is first connected, current will flow through the two diodes, D1 and D2, and the 2k2 resistor R1. Each diode will maintain a 0.6v forward voltage, so the base of transistor TR1 will be held 1.2v below the supply voltage. This will bring TR1 into conduction. Remember that a pnp transistor turns on when the base is negative of the emitter. TR1 will draw current through the 2R2 resistor R2, which will therefore drop some of the supply voltage. Once it drops 0.6v, equilibrium is reached, since any further current through R2 would mean that the TR1's base–to–emitter voltage would drop below 0.6v, which would tend to turn it off. The current at which the 2R2 resistor drops 0.6v is given by Ohm's law,

$$I = V/R = 0.6/2.2 = 0.27A.$$

Therefore, 0.27A of emitter to collector current flows through TR1. This begins to charge up the capacitor C2, and the voltage on the positive plate of C2 starts to rise towards +18v. How long will this take? We can use the capacitor formula, $Q = CV$ to find the charge stored in C2. Let us suppose we have used 10,000μF for C2.

$$Q = CV = 0.01 \times 18 = 0.18 \ coulomb$$

Now, this charge is stored at a rate of 0.27A by the current through TR1. We know that Q = It, so the time taken is,

$$t = Q/I = 0.18/0.27 = 0.66 \ second$$

Thus a little over half a second after the +18v supply is turned on, our capacitor is fully charged. We can now apply this fully charged capacitor across one or other of our solenoid coils, using a push–button switch, or an 'electric pencil'. The latter is simply a length of brass rod soldered to a flying lead, which we can use to touch the heads of brass screws on the control panel. We have already seen that the typical resistance of the solenoid coil is only around three ohms, so the application of +18v would cause a coil current of around 6A – ample current to operate the solenoid. However, as soon as this 6A starts to flow, the voltage on C2 will drop as it discharges. Therefore, the 6A current will not flow for long. We can work out roughly how long if we assume, as it starts at 6A and drops to zero, that the average value of the discharge current is 3A. To get rid of 0.18 coulomb at a rate of 3A (remember a current is a rate of flow of charge) will take,

$$t = Q/I = 0.18/3 = 0.06 \ second$$

Now, this is plenty of time for the solenoid plunger to move, but not enough to cause any significant heating of the coil.

Once the capacitor has discharged, and the push–button is opened, the circuitry around TR1 will start to charge it up again, and in 0.66 sec, the circuit will once again be ready for operation. If the push–button is stuck, or we leave the electric pencil in position too long, the capacitor will not fully re–charge, as the 0.27A charging current will simply flow through the coil, producing a power dissipation of less than a quarter of a watt.

Notice that, although we have provided a 6A operating current to the solenoid, at no time has the current from the 18v supply exceeded 0.27A. It might seem that we have got something for nothing, but this is not so. Remember that charging the capacitor took 0.66 sec, during which time a current of 0.27A flowed into it. The 6A current that came out of the unit to

operate the solenoid lasted only a fraction of a second. In this case, the capacitor has acted like a piggy bank. It takes a long time to fill it, but smash it open and the money's all there at once!

A Driver Circuit

Discharging the capacitor C2 directly via a push–button switch is not an ideal method. Its main disadvantage is that normally we will want the push–button on some sort of control panel and the solenoid at some distance from it on the layout. We will need several feet of wire between them, and this wire will carry the full discharge current of C2. It will therefore need to be heavy duty cable, to avoid excessive voltage drop, and long runs of heavy duty cable are bulky and require expensive connectors between layout and control panel. In addition, the push switch will be subject to some very high instantaneous currents, which will not be good for it.

The circuitry in fig 18 overcomes these problems. The discharge current for each coil is now routed through transistors TR1 and TR2. These are turned on whenever base current flows. This time, we have used npn transistors, so anytime the base is above +0.6v collector current will flow. The transistor type used, TIP131, has a very high current gain, over 1,000. Therefore to turn on the full 6A discharge current through the coil requires only a few mA. We can therefore position the solenoid driver and capacitor discharge units close to the solenoid, and the cable runs from the control panel can use very thin wire and inexpensive connectors.

Whenever input 1L or 2L is taken to +12v, transistor TR1 will conduct, throwing the solenoid plunger to the left. When input 1R or 2R is taken to +12v, transistor TR2 will conduct, throwing the plunger to the right. The diodes D1–D4 isolate these inputs from each other. The remaining diodes, D5–D8, are there to protect the transistors and C2 from voltage spikes arising from the current pulse through the solenoid coil. These occur

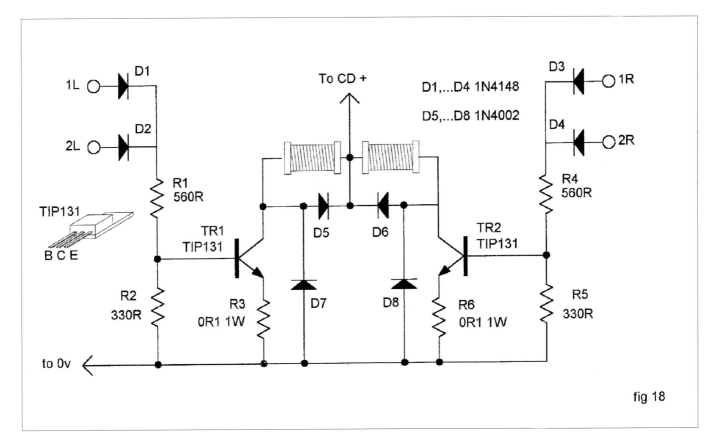

fig 18

whenever a large current is turned either on or off in a coil and can reach quite high voltages.

Remember to connect the 0v terminal of your CD unit, and the 0v terminal of the +12v supply from which the inputs 1L,2L... are driven, otherwise you will not have a complete circuit for the base current of TR1 and TR2.

Route Selection

The circuit we have just discussed can be used to provide a route selection facility. In fig 18, we have shown just two inputs to set the point left and two to set it right. In principle, however, you could have more than this. By wiring several of these inputs to a single push–button, you could have that button set a whole series of points either left or right, according to which route you want to select.

If you are using the Trax program, you will find a simple example of push–button routing. This is my very first '0' gauge layout, and it is in the file

'whitchurch1.trx'. If you look at the properties of point P1 (right–click on it and select 'properties') you will find that its normal setting is 'Left' and that its 'Setting change' rule is 'B3,B4;B1,B2'. This is a short–hand way of saying 'change the setting from normal if B3 or B4 is pressed; restore it to normal if either B1 or B2 are pressed'. If you now put the Trax program into 'Test/Operate' mode you will find that the points switch according to the push–buttons, and that power is fed to the appropriate sidings in turn.

Obviously, this is a very simple route selection scheme. You can build up far more extensive ones, with more sophisticated operating rules. This type of layout is useful for storage sidings, marshalling yards and the like. We mentioned in chapter 1 that three–way points need care in operating them, in case the switches are damaged by trying to force them into an impossible position. Route setting offers one way of overcoming this. Three buttons could

select each of the three possible ways through the point and set the tie–bars appropriately.

You should note that the capacitor C2 in fig 17 might need to be increased in size for more complex schemes. If C2 is feeding two solenoid coils, it will discharge twice as quickly, in other words in 0.03 sec instead of 0.06 sec. If you added a third, it would discharge in an even shorter time. The more solenoids you drive off a single capacitor, the shorter the time for which their coils are energised. Eventually a point is reached where the current 'pulse' through the coil is over too quickly to operate the point. One way to overcome this is to use a much larger value of capacitance for C2, or to add further capacitors in parallel with it. This will increase the recharging time proportionally. Alternatively, you could use additional capacitor discharge units, and spread the load around them. Try to decide which points will most often be required to

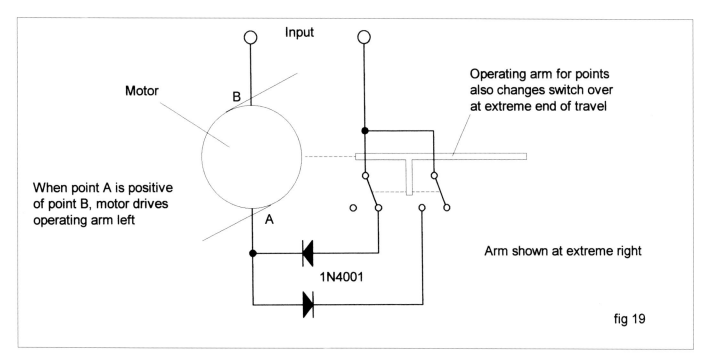

Input

Motor

B

Operating arm for points also changes switch over at extreme end of travel

When point A is positive of point B, motor drives operating arm left

A

1N4001

Arm shown at extreme right

fig 19

switch simultaneously, and keep these on separate units. In the case of Whitchurch Mk I, I used a separate CD unit on each of the three baseboards where there were points to be operated. This meant that no one unit had to switch more than two points simultaneously.

Point Motor Operation

As has been mentioned, some modellers dislike the loud 'clunk' and rapid motion of the point switch blades associated with the use of solenoids. Therefore, we now turn to the use of 'slow–motion' point motors. These provide the necessary motion over a period of a second or two rather than a few milliseconds, which looks rather more realistic. They do tend to replace the clunk by a high–pitched whine, however, which can be equally distracting!

Point motors are generally operated by either toggle switches or microswitches operated by a lever frame, rather than by push–button switches. This is useful, because the position of the switch dolly, or the lever, gives an indication of the point setting. If the point is not easily visible, the setting can be difficult to see.

The point motor is usually equipped with a circuit such as that shown in fig 19, which ensures that, at each end of the travel, the appropriate diode is cut out, thus preventing further movement in that direction.

The motor has just two terminals, and there are two schemes for operating it. In the first scheme, a single polarity 12v supply is used to feed power via a double–pole switch, which enables its polarity to be reversed. This method has the advantage of requiring only a single power supply, but two wires will need to go to every point motor from the control panel. If the points or signals are to be operated by a lever frame, using a microswitch under each lever, this scheme may prove difficult. This is because double–pole microswitches are not easy to find, so you may need to use two single–pole microswitches. An alternative scheme is to hold one terminal of the motor permanently at 0v, and to switch the other to either +12v or –12v. Suitable voltages can be obtained from the dual voltage power supply described in the previous chapter.

Typical current requirement for such a motor is in the 100–200mA region, so a 1A supply should drive several.

Remember that current is only drawn whilst the motor is in motion, so even if you have a great many points and signals, you need only accommodate the number of motors that you can expect to operate simultaneously.

Some modellers prefer a lower voltage than 12v to operate their motors. This gives a lower operating speed, and reduces motor current. Most motors are designed to operate on a range of voltages, e.g. 6–14v. You could readily change the voltage supplied by the dual polarity supply described in the last chapter by using a 7808 and a 7908 instead of the 7812 and 7912. This would give ±8v instead of ±12v.

Route Selection Using Point Motors

The point motor scheme is very straightforward if one switch or lever controls just one point or signal. It is advisable to standardise on a scheme whereby if the point is to be reversed from its normal setting, or a signal put to danger, a voltage of +12v is fed to it. To return the setting to normal, a voltage of –12v is used. (or 8v, or 6v or whatever you choose). Thus when a lever is reversed or a switch is clicked 'on', it provides +12v. In the normal or 'off'

Lever	Sets Normal	Sets Reverse
1	18,19,20,21	–
2	–	22
3	–	22
4	22	–
5	22	–
6	18,19	17
7	19,20,21	18
8	–	20,21
9	–	–
10	19,20,21	18
11	21	20,22
12	–	22
13	18,19	17
14	–	–
15	17,18	19
16	22	–

position, it provides –12v.

It is equally easy to have one lever operate several points. For example, a crossover in a double track main line consists of two points. We will always want the two points to be set for either the 'straight on' or the 'crossover' direction. Therefore, we can supply the two point motors from the same switch or lever, as we will always want them to be either both at +12v or both at –12v.

A problem occurs, however, with a route selection scheme. Here we may want a given lever or switch to set some points in their normal direction, others to be reversed. This means that some will need to be fed with +12v, and some with –12v, from the same lever.

Fig 20 illustrates a simple relay circuit which overcomes this problem. The levers or toggle switches still supply +12v when reversed, as before. This time, however, we allow for two kinds of input to the point motor. In one kind of input (labelled 1R, 2R, 3R) reversing the lever reverses the point and in the other kind of input (labelled 1N, 2N, 3N) reversing the lever sets the point to normal. Further diodes can be added as required.

An interesting scheme of this type was introduced in 1922 at Winchester Chesil station, on the Didcot, Newbury and Southampton Railway. This was one of the very first attempts at a proper route selection scheme. The signalling scheme is described in detail in *'Winchester (Great Western) a Snapshot in Time'* by Kevin Robertson (KRB Publications). However, the table on this page, summarises the main features insofar as point setting is concerned. Each of the 16 levers operates a signal controlling a particular train movement, and each movement involves a series of points to be set normal or reverse.

Let us takes as an example point 18. This, as can be seen from the table, is to be reversed if either lever 7 or lever 10 is reversed, and it is to be set normal if any of levers 1, 6, 13 or 15 is reversed. Assuming we stick to our convention that a lever provides (via its microswitch) +12v if it is reversed, then we would simply use

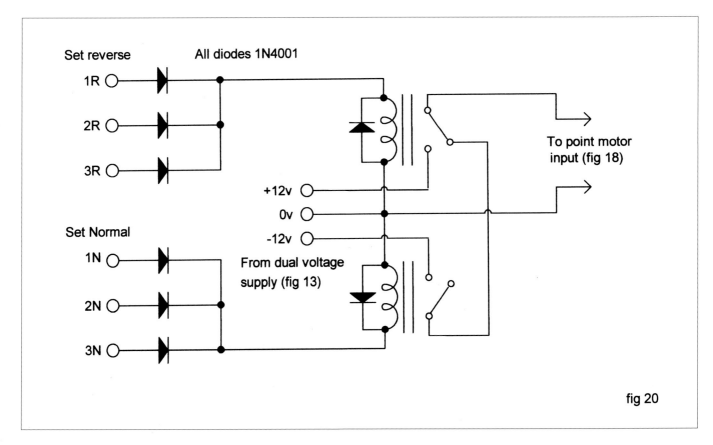

fig 20

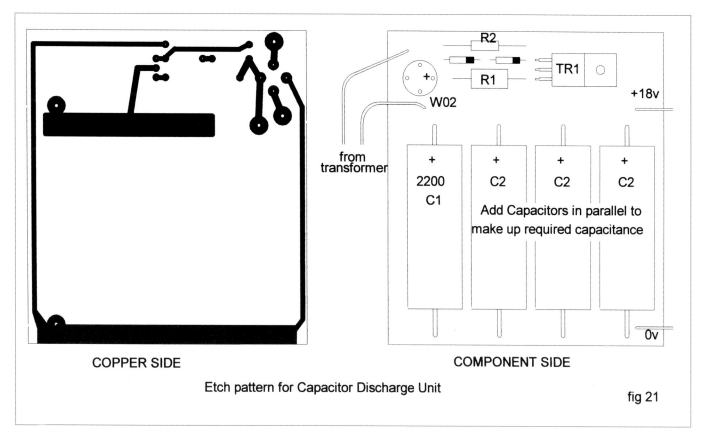

COPPER SIDE

COMPONENT SIDE

Etch pattern for Capacitor Discharge Unit

fig 21

a point motor supplied by a circuit such as that in fig 20 with levers 7 and 10 wired to 1R and 2R, and levers 1, 6, 13 and 15 wired to 1N, 2N, 3N and 4N (note that we need an extra diode for this). Similar arrangements would apply to the point motors for points 19, 20, 21 and 22. If you are using Trax, you will find a file 'chesil.trx' which demonstrates one possible way of implementing a route setting scheme based on Chesil, together with switching for no less than four controllers.

Diamond Crossings

We mentioned in chapter 1 that the diamond crossing was an unfortunate piece of trackwork from the operating point of view, in that it has no moving parts, yet needs an electrical switch. If you are trying to operate your model based on full–size practice, i.e. with levers to operate points and signals and to control electrical switching almost as an aside, then the diamond stands out like a sore

thumb! It has no moving parts, yet requires a lever to operate it!

You may be able to build the switching into the circuitry for operating nearby points. If access to the diamond is from an adjacent point, then the operating mechanism for this point could incorporate the necessary switching for the diamond, as well as for its own crossing vee.

On occasion, you may find that the track switching for surrounding points automatically switches the diamond crossing vees. There is an example of such a situation on my Whitchurch Mk III layout. If you are using Trax, open file 'whitchurch3.trx', go into Test/Operate mode and zoom in on the station area. Reverse levers 4, 6 and 7 on the station lever frame, and you will see that the polarity of the diamond crossing vees takes care of itself. This is, however, not always possible.

Memory Wire

Mention should be made of another

possibility for operating points and signals, the use of so–called memory wire, such as Nitinol, a nickel–titanium alloy. This is a member of an extraordinary group of materials which exhibit the so–called 'shape memory effect'. At low temperatures Nitinol has a needle–like crystalline structure that can easily be deformed, for example by bending or stretching. Above around 100°C the crystalline structure is cubic, and if the material has been bent or stretched this sets up stresses which cause it to return to its 'remembered' shape.

To operate points or signals from such wire, you fix one end of it in position, and attach the other end to a spring which puts it under tension. The attachment between wire and spring is made, for example, by bolting them to some kind of operating arm such as a crank. To work the point or signal, you need to pass enough current through the wire to cause it to heat itself to over 100°. It will then shrink, causing the operating arm to move. When the

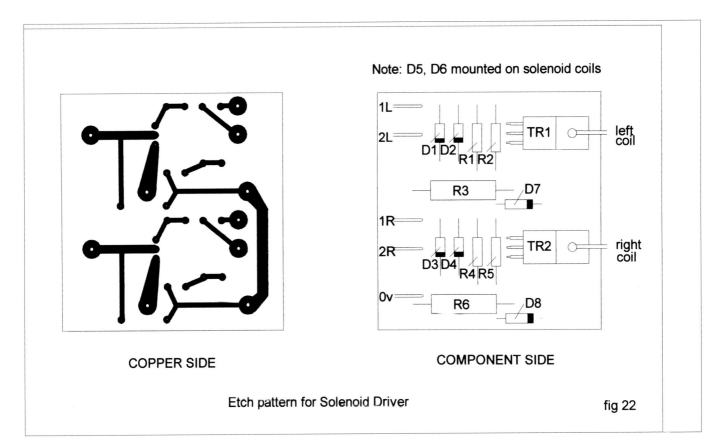

Note: D5, D6 mounted on solenoid coils

COPPER SIDE

COMPONENT SIDE

Etch pattern for Solenoid Driver

fig 22

current ceases, the wire cools and returns to its stretched length under the influence of the spring. Deformation is around 3–5%, so to get a shrinkage of 3mm, you should use about 100mm length of wire.

The requisite heating current is in the 200–400mA region, so if you ran this from a 12v regulated supply, as described in the previous chapter, you would need a total resistance of between 30 and 60 ohms. The wire itself has a resistance of around 5 ohms for a 100mm length, so an external series resistor between 25 and 55 ohms will be required. Power in the resistor will be around 4W so a 5W rating should be regarded as the minimum. If you operated a lot of points in this way, the current requirements could get large.

Although I have purchased an experimenter's kit, I have not (yet) used this in a layout and am not therefore qualified to comment on its effectiveness. However, it does seem to offer extremely interesting possibilities.

The superb LBSCR design signal box on Michael Ball's 'Ferring'. Whilst it is perfectly feasible to place the control panel near to the actual signal box on the layout this may not always be desirable or sometimes practicable.

Chapter 5
TRACK FEEDS and BREAKS

We have now discussed a range of electronic circuits which can be used to operate the points, crossings and signals of the layout from a control panel or lever frame. As was mentioned in chapter one, ideally these should be the only parts of the layout that are overtly controlled. Full–size railways don't have track feeds, so if we want to operate our model as closely as possible to full–size practice, we should try to avoid making them obvious.

Wherever possible, therefore, the setting of points and signals should determine the status of feeds and breaks on the layout. By *status*, we mean, for a track feed, 'to which controller (if any) is it connected?' For a track break, we mean 'is the gap bridged or not?' By changing the *status* of feeds and breaks, we determine the *scope* of each controller at any given time. Our goal is to use the setting of points and signals for a given movement to set the scope for the appropriate controller to make that movement.

The location and rules for setting the status of track feeds and breaks are therefore absolutely crucial to the running of the railway. How do we determine where they should be, and what their operating rules should be?

Locating Feeds and Breaks

The first step is to decide on your operating strategy. Is the layout to be worked by a single operator? If there are to be more than one, where should they be situated, what areas does the layout naturally break down into? The answers to these questions will determine the number of controllers required and their scope. In breaking the layout up in this way, geographical considerations are not the only ones to bear in mind, indeed others may be more important. A key deciding factor is to identify where it would make sense to have two locomotives in motion simultaneously. In a layout that had two terminus stations, it might seem at first sight that a controller

attached to each station, whose scope was the station itself would be the logical arrangement. However, we have already referred to the advantage of having the operator who stops a train control it from the start of its journey. For a two–terminus layout, then, it might make more sense to have the controllers' scope as the outbound platform(s) of the station at the far end of the line and the inbound platform(s) of the station at the local end.

You will then have to decide on the location of track breaks and feeds for each controller, to ensure that all desired movements are possible, without the possibility of short–circuits between different controller terminals.

Within the scope of each controller, there will often be a group of lines that can be regarded as exclusive. No other controllers will need access to them, so you can decide on the feed location(s) to serve these. The next step will be to decide where there need to be track breaks to isolate the controllers from each other. Ignore, for the moment, the fact that trains will require to run over these track breaks. Simply position them so that the controllers do not interfere with each other.

Now you must decide what movements *between* the scope of different controllers are required, and how they are to be achieved. For example, in the case of the two–terminus layout, there must be some way in which an arrival can be turned round and put onto the departure platform. It will then come under the scope of the other controller. In the simplest case, you could achieve this by simply giving control of both scopes to one controller. However, this would mean, in this example, that if a train were being turned around at one station, the same thing couldn't be happening at the other, which would be a disadvantage. Therefore, you will more often want to transfer control of only a part of the scope. This will require that you isolate these parts with further track breaks, and install feeds which can be switched from one controller to the other.

Introducing Logic

To do this, we introduce the concept of *rules* governing the operation of track feeds and breaks. A rule might be a simple one such as 'toggle switch S1 is ON', or a more complex one such as 'EITHER the up platform starter signal, OR the goods loop to up main signal, OR the up starter from down platform signal are OFF'. Such rules can become rather complicated, involving logical conditions and the like. For example, in my Whitchurch Mk III layout the feed at the station entrance (Feed A) has a controller 1 operating rule which reads 'L1&–L8,L9&–L2,L3'. This is shorthand for 'connect this feed to controller number 1 if EITHER lever 1 is reversed AND lever 8 is NOT reversed, OR if lever 9 is reversed and lever 2 is NOT reversed, OR if lever 3 is reversed'. Lever 1 is the up home signal, 2 is the up starter from the station platform. We normally want an up train entering the station to be under the control of the station controller. However, if the up starter (8) is also pulled, then this is a through train and we therefore want it to be controlled by the storage siding operator on controller 2 (since this is where it will stop). The arrangements for down through trains (levers 2 and 9) are similar. Lever 3 is the shunt signal, which grants access to the main line for shunting purposes, but only as far as the break half–way round the curve. Here, there is a track break whose operating rule reads 'L1,L2' which means 'bridge across this track break if lever 1 OR lever 2 are pulled'. Thus for up or down main line trains the gap will be bridged, but if lever 3 is pulled it will not, so shunting can only proceed as far as this point. In full–size practice we would have a sign here saying 'Limit of Shunt'.

The operating rules for a track feed or break are examples of very simple *logical expressions*. Now, it may seem like overkill to get involved in symbolic logic, just to decide where to feed power to your model railway, but logical expressions do have one enormous advantage. They must adhere strictly to a set of rules of syntax if they are to be interpreted correctly, and this forces us to think logically about what we want to achieve. Also, as we shall see shortly, if proper logical expressions are used to define our rules, then their translation into wiring diagrams becomes straightforward. The expressions may contain one or more of the three *logical operators*, AND (represented in shorthand form by the ampersand character), OR (represented by a comma) and NOT (represented by a minus sign). The rest of the expression consists of names of levers or switches on the control panel, which we call *logical variables*. Logical expressions are evaluated according to a strict order of precedence, which is:

First, the logical variables are evaluated. In our case, this means that if a switch or lever is in its OFF, or normal (starting) position, the value of its logical variable is FALSE. If the switch is ON or the lever is pulled to its reverse position the value of the corresponding logical variable is TRUE.

Next, the NOT operators are evaluated. The logic here is that the variable named after the minus sign, representing NOT, has its value negated. In the above example, the term '–L8' appears. If lever 8 were pulled, then L8 would be TRUE, so '–L8' would be FALSE. If lever 8 were in its normal position, then L8 would be FALSE, so '–L8' would be TRUE.

Thirdly, the AND operators are evaluated. The logic for these, as their name implies, is that all of the logical variables (negated where appropriate) connected by the AND operators must be TRUE for the result to be true. Thus, 'L4&L6&L7' would be TRUE if and only if all three of L4, L6 and L7 were TRUE, i.e. reversed (if they were levers).

Fourthly, and finally, the OR operators are evaluated. The logic here is that the result will be TRUE if any one of the alternatives is TRUE. Thus, 'L4,L6,L7' would be true if any one of the three levers were pulled.

Logic Implementation

There are many ways in which these rules can be realised in practice. One of the most obvious would be to use the vast range of integrated circuits manufactured for the computer industry. One can buy very cheaply logic IC packages containing several AND, OR or NOT circuits, together with a whole host of more complex ones.

Several layouts that have been built successfully using such logic ICs, however they do have some drawbacks. One of the most popular families of IC logic runs on a 5v supply, and most model railways use a 12v supply. It is therefore necessary to introduce a second power supply voltage. Logic ICs are also very susceptible to things like voltage spikes, and model railway engines are exceptionally good at making such spikes. Every time an engine runs over a dirty bit of track or loses contact with the rail at a crossing vee, a spark will occur and induce a voltage spike into the logic circuit. I built one experimental set–up which employed a small memory device whose response to such spikes was spontaneously to reverse the polarity of supply to the track! At the end of the chain of logic will be a relay or a point motor, and a logic IC cannot normally supply enough current to drive one of these. A relay driver circuit will therefore be required.

If some relays are needed anyway, it seems sensible to use relays to implement all of the logic, as well as the actual driving of the point motors etc. Therefore, all of my layouts have ended up using relays for logic implementation. This may seem somewhat old–hat, but relays do have a number of additional advantages, not the least of which is that you can hear them operate, and (if you use the ones encased in clear plastic) you can see whether they are energised or not. This make fault diagnosis a great deal easier than with logic ICs whose operation is both silent and invisible.

We will therefore proceed on the basis of using 12v relays to implement our logic, and we will follow the convention established in the last chapter that when a switch or lever is in its normal position, it will provide a control voltage of 12v, and when it is reversed, or clicked ON, it will provide +12v. Thus, in our implementation, we must represent the logical value TRUE by +12v and the value FALSE by 12v. We will therefore need a ±12v supply, as described in chapter 3.

Relay Logic

In fig 23 are three circuits which represent the basic logic functions AND, OR and NOT. Fig 23 (a) is a circuit which provides an output corresponding to the NOT logical operator. That is, if the input is TRUE the output is FALSE, and if the input is FALSE, the output is TRUE. A TRUE input would correspond to +12v. This would flow through the diode, thence through the relay coil, and the relay contact would switch to the 12v position (relays are always shown on circuit diagrams in the unenergised position), giving a 12v output. If the input were at 12v , D1 would not conduct, the relay would be unenergised, and the output would be connected to +12v. We have therefore reproduced the function of the NOT logical operator, as required.

The diode connected 'in reverse' across the relay coil is there to protect against voltage spikes, in the same way as those across the solenoid coils in fig 18. It is always a good idea to include protection diodes like this across coils which will be subject to large current pulses. Not only will this prolong the life of the component, but it will reduce interference with nearby TV and radio sets.

Fig 23 (b) presents a relay circuit that provides the logical AND function. Remember that the AND function takes two inputs, and provides a TRUE output if both of the two inputs are TRUE. One of the inputs, A, is connected as before to a relay via a diode, thus the relay will be energised if this input A is at +12v, i.e. TRUE. If A is at 12v , i.e. FALSE the relay is unenergised and the output is connected to 12v , irrespective of the value of the second input, B. However, if A is at +12v, the output will be the same as B, i.e. +12v if B is TRUE, 12v if it is FALSE. Thus the output will be TRUE only if both inputs A and B are true. The circuit reproduces exactly the AND function we require. If more than two logical variables are to be ANDed together, we can simply use a series of similar circuits strung in series, taking the output of one circuit to form input B of the next.

Fig 23(c) is a circuit to provide the OR function. Here, we use two input diodes, connected to the two inputs A and B. If the anode of either one of these is at +12v, representing a TRUE value for one of the variables, then the relay will be energised, connecting the output to +12v. If both inputs are at 12v, then neither of the diodes will conduct, the relay will be unenergised and the output will remain connected to 12v, exactly as we require for the OR function. If more than two variables are to be ORed together, simply use more input diodes.

Using combinations of these circuits we can reproduce in electronic terms any of the logical expressions that we require to control power feeds and track breaks to our layout. For example, fig 24 represents

a combination of AND, OR and NOT circuits that reproduce the function 'L1&–L8,L9&–L2,L3' that we met earlier. You should trace the circuit through and convince yourself that it does actually provide the logic required.

Simplification

It may well be that a one–for–one translation of our logical expression into relay circuits ends up using more relays than are strictly necessary. For example, if a particular track feed were to be connected in all circumstances except when lever 8 were pulled, then we would end up with the lever providing 12v in its 'normal' position, feeding a NOT circuit which turned this 12v into +12v, the latter then being used to control the feed. We could achieve this same result by simply reversing the polarity of the output from lever 8, thereby saving a relay, or by having the relay that controls the feed operate on 12v instead of +12v.

However, much caution should be exercised when going down this route. In general, there is a lot to be said for standardising. Hopefully, you will not get involved in maintenance work on any given circuit more than once every few years. If you have made arbitrary changes

to the wiring conventions, you will almost certainly have forgotten what they were and fault–fixing will become that much harder. Relays are not that expensive, and the use of a few extra in the interest of standardisation is not a high price to pay.

There are, however, areas where you could sensibly make things simpler. Recall that in our OR circuit, the use of a relay after the input diodes enables us to have an output which is at either +12v (for TRUE) or 12v (for FALSE). Now, these voltages are only strictly necessary if we are driving a point motor, where +12v will put the point in its reverse position, 12v will restore it to normal. If, instead of a point motor, we are using the OR circuit to control connection to a track feed or break, then only the +12v is of any interest. Therefore, we can dispense with the relay, and simply take the output from the junction of the diodes marked 'X' in fig 23.

Another possible simplification is to 'share' logic between different parts of the layout. The translation of our operating rule into logic circuits has been on a completely independent, rule–by–rule basis. Now, this means that if a particular condition crops up in many different rules it will be duplicated. For example 'lever 1

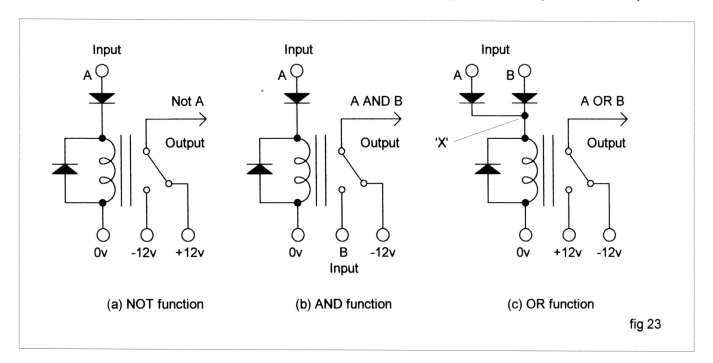

(a) NOT function   (b) AND function   (c) OR function

fig 23

AND NOT lever 8' might be used in three different places on the layout. A rule–by–rule implementation of the logic would mean that six relays were used where two would do. In this case, provided it were clearly labelled under the baseboard, the function could be calculated once, using two relays, then taken to the three separate circuits where it was needed.

Connecting Up

We come now to the 'business end' of our chain of logic. We have a network of relays and diodes which take our lever or switch settings and make the logical connections between them by means of logic circuits. The output of these logic circuits must now be used to determine the scope of each the controllers.

For track breaks, the 'business end' of the logic circuit it relatively simple. Some breaks, of course, will be permanent. For example, those in ovals to prevent short circuits, as in fig 6, do not require any logic as they are never

bridged. However, where a break has been introduced to separate the scope of two controllers, then it must be bridged whenever one or other controller's scope is to be extended over the break. This will simply be a matter of connecting the rail on the two sides of the break, using a double–pole relay if the break is in both rails, or a single–pole relay if only in one. The relay drive can come directly from one of our OR logic circuits, picking it up from point 'X' (fig 24) if desired. Fig 25 illustrates how we would wire a relay to bridge either a single or double break, wiring the 'common' to one side and the 'normally open' to the other side of the break.

In the case of a feed, we need one double–pole relay for each controller that might be potentially connected to the feed. For each relay the two 'normally open' contacts are connected to a controller, and the 'normally closed' contacts are daisy–chained as shown in fig 26, which represents a feed point with potential

connection to four controllers. Such an arrangement avoids a short–circuit between controllers if the logic for two different controllers evaluates to TRUE (it shouldn't, but these things can happen). If logic circuit 'A' (which might, for example, be the output of fig 24) evaluates to TRUE then the feed point is connected to controller 1 output. If logic circuit 'B' is TRUE (and A is FALSE) it is connected to controller 2 and so on.

My preference is to place the relay logic circuits under the baseboard, adjacent to the feeds, breaks, points and signals they control. The connection between control panel and baseboard is thereby limited to a single wire for each lever/switch, plus a common '0v', and a pair of wires for each controller. Thus, if you had a 9–lever frame, and 1 controller, you might need 12–way connectors. However, you may need fewer. If you situate the control panel/lever frame on or near a part of the layout where a large number of points,

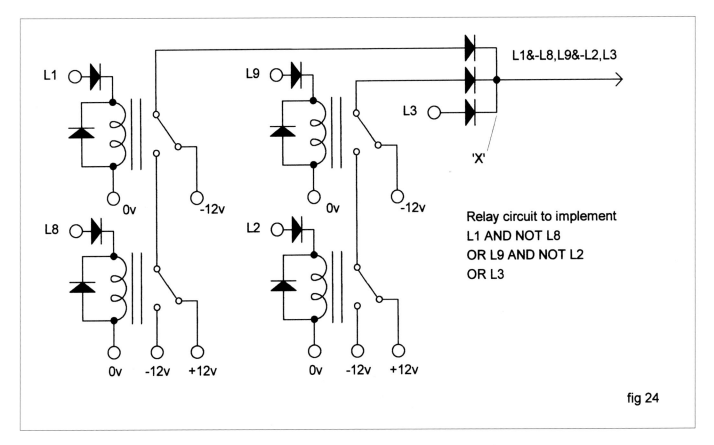

L1&-L8,L9&-L2,L3

Relay circuit to implement
L1 AND NOT L8
OR L9 AND NOT L2
OR L3

fig 24

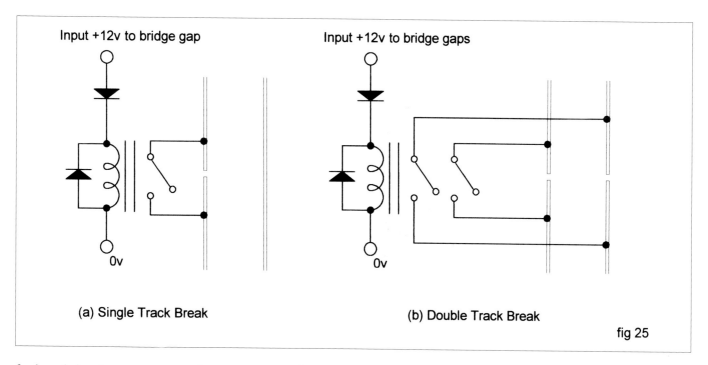

Input +12v to bridge gap

Input +12v to bridge gaps

0v

0v

(a) Single Track Break

(b) Double Track Break

fig 25

feeds and signals are concentrated, you may find that most of the control signals are required only locally, and the longer cable runs might involve only one or two separate wires.

Relay Circuit Boards

The reader will notice that there are no PCB etch patterns for relay logic boards. Relays, unlike other components must have mounting holes drilled in *exactly* the right position. The PCB layout must therefore be made for a specific relay make and model.

Manual Testing

There are many possible approaches to testing your track design. The first is, don't bother! Design the layout, form a rough idea about wiring, build the layout then set about finding the short–circuits and dead sections by trial and error. When you find a short circuit, try to work out where you need a track break and put one in. Where you find a dead section, put in another feed and try to work out how to switch it. Although haphazard and unworkmanlike, this approach can be fun, especially for those who enjoy detective work!

If you want to adopt a more structured approach, it is first necessary to draw out the layout on a reasonably large sheet of paper. Draw it with both rails shown, and with all track breaks represented as gaps, including those on points and crossings. Then go round the whole thing and assign a number or letter to each section of electrically continuous rail. By electrically continuous, we mean that you can trace around the whole of the section of rail without having to jump any gaps. Note also that such sections should have either two ends or no ends. If you find any other number, then you've gone wrong somewhere. The most likely cause is failing to take account of gaps in the closure rails of points (see chapter 1). To avoid this pitfall, draw your points without switch or closure rails, as in fig 27.

Next, decide on what movements you want to allow, and how (if at all) these are to be signalled. Ever since I first had the pleasure of operating on John Shaw's Aveton Gifford layout, I have been convinced that controlling the track using signal levers is the only way to do it. It's how the real thing works, and as such gives a much more authentic air to the whole layout. It is not necessary to have every signal modelled. Indeed, on my own Whitchurch model the 'signals' controlling the movements on the storage siding baseboards are entirely virtual. These baseboards stack flat, so there's no room for signals. Nevertheless, the levers are there so operation still has a suitably authentic feel. Draw up a large table, with a column for each lever, both signals and points, then a column for each track feed, and finally one for each continuous track section.

Then, for each movement, go through the track sections and decide which controller they are to be connected to. For example, in the first line of the table in fig 27, with no levers pulled, we have decided to power each station from its own controller, and leave the central track length 'dead'. Therefore, we want sections 'a' and 'b' connected to controller 1 'live', c to controller 1 'return', and similarly for sections 'f','g' and 'h'. These are shown in fig 27 as '1L','1R', etc. Then, write the controller number under each feed that will give you the connections required. In fig 27, this is shown as controller number 1 under feed F1, and controller 2 under feed F3.

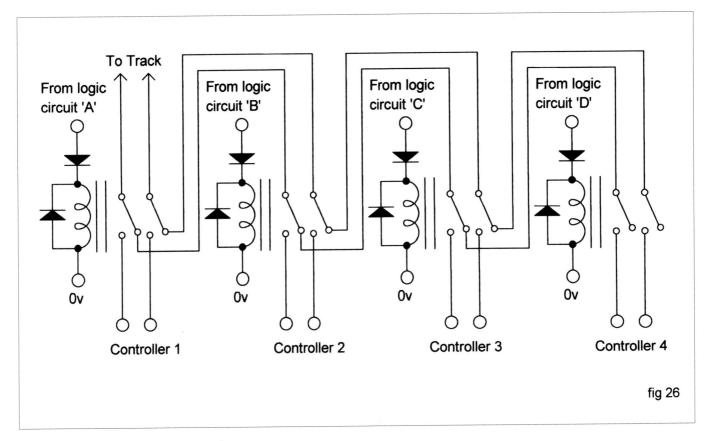

fig 26

Repeat this process for each movement. For example, in the second line on fig 27, we have pulled station A's starter. We therefore take away control over station A from controller 1, as we want the operator stopping the train (controller 2) to control it. However, we do not yet assign control to the other controller. He may not be ready, possibly because he is still shunting in station B. Once 2 has pulled his home signal, as in fig 27 line 3, we hand control over the whole line to 2, who can now drive the train out of A and on towards B. Once the train has passed A's starter signal, we can return that to danger, and restore controller 1's power to feed F1. Shunting in A could now proceed, if for example there were another engine stored on the siding. This is the situation represented by line 4.

Repeat this procedure for all the movements you foresee and you will end up with a table like that in fig 27. Now you need to look carefully down the central columns and try to identify some logical rules for connecting the controller feeds. For example, you notice that feed F1 is connected to controller 1 except when A's starter is off. The rule for connecting feed F1 to controller 1 could therefore be '–L2'. Likewise, you observe that the same feed is connected to controller 2 only when both A's starter and B's home signals are off. Thus, the rule for connecting controller 2 to F1 could be 'L2&K3', these being the levers operating the appropriate signals.

You can now define the complete rule for feed F1 as 'controller 1 if –L2, controller 2 if L2&K3'. These can then be implemented using a 'NOT' and an 'AND' circuit, as in fig 23, providing the two logic circuit inputs to a controller feed circuit, similar to that in fig 26, but with only two relays as we only have two controllers. A similar rule will accomplish the necessary at station B. For feed F2 we require the minimum of logic. All that is necessary is a controller feed circuit with just two relays, and the logic inputs to these come directly from the levers L3 and K3.

Having gone through all the 'planned' movements, you now need to decide whether any problems would exist if signals and points were set for 'unplanned' movements. To be thorough, you would need to consider every possible combination of lever settings (and with six levers there are 64 of these) and apply the logic for track feeds and breaks to every one of them, checking whether any given feed could be connected to more than one controller, or whether a given controller could be short–circuited.

Even with a small track plan, this is somewhat tedious. With a large one it becomes a real bind. This was the point at which the idea of Trax was conceived. By using a computer to evaluate all the logic and make all the appropriate connections, the process can be greatly speeded up.

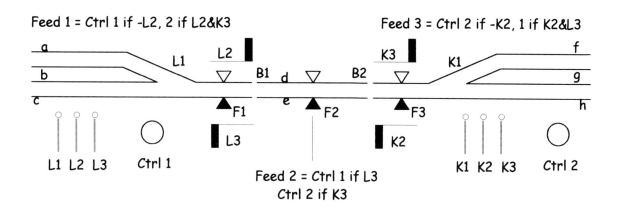

Station A Station B

Feed 1 = Ctrl 1 if -L2, 2 if L2&K3

Feed 3 = Ctrl 2 if -K2, 1 if K2&L3

Feed 2 = Ctrl 1 if L3
Ctrl 2 if K3

Lever Settings						Feed			Power to .. Track Section							
L1	L2	L3	K1	K2	K3	F1	F2	F3	a	b	c	d	e	f	g	h
-	-	-	-	-	-	1	-	2	1L	1L	1R	-	-	2L	2L	2R
-	X	-	-	-	-	-	-	2	-	-	-	-	-	2L	2L	2R
-	X	-	-	-	X	2	2	2	2L	2L	2R	2L	2R	2L	2L	2R
-	-	-	-	-	X	1	2	2	1L	1L	1R	2L	2R	2L	2L	2R
-	-	-	-	X	-	1	-	-	1L	1L	1R	-	-	-	-	-
-	-	X	-	X	-	1	1	1	1L	1L	1R	1L	1R	1L	1L	1R
-	-	X	-	-	-	1	1	2	1L	1L	1R	1L	1R	2L	2L	2R
X	-	-	-	-	-	1	-	2	1L	1R	1R	-	-	2L	2L	2R
X	X	-	-	-	-	-	-	2	-	-	-	-	-	2L	2L	2R
X	X	-	-	-	X	2	2	2	2L	2R	2R	2L	2R	2L	2L	2R
X	-	-	-	-	X	1	2	2	1L	1R	1R	2L	2R	2L	2L	2R

etc., etc., etc...

fig 27

47

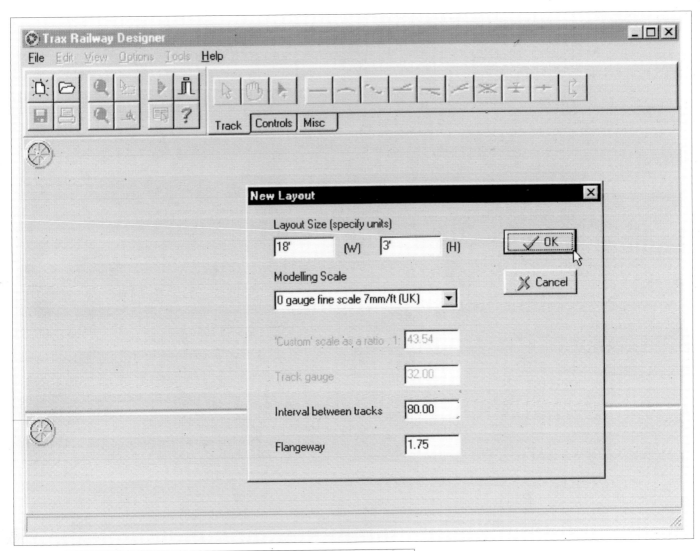

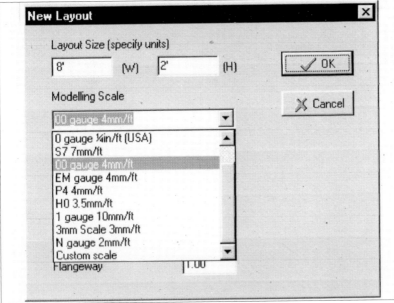

Getting started with TRAX.

From FILE first select NEW and then define the size of room you have available.
Although shown here in 'feet', the programme will work equally well with metres / centimetres. TRAX will always draw a rectangle of squares so if you are working in a 'L' shape or require an operating space in the centre of your layout, take care not to place sidings or running lines in that location!

The scale is also variable to include all well known and readily available scales and gauges and even the facility to customise an individual requirement.

Chapter 6

GETTING STARTED WITH TRAX

For the final chapter, we will take a more detailed look at Trax, and use it to create a working model of the small layout discussed at the end of the previous chapter. You may find it helpful to refer to the colour plate in the centre–fold of the book, which highlights the various toolbuttons referred to in the text. If you get stuck, there is a sample layout file called 'started.trx' which represents what your layout should look like. If you save your own example, take care not to give it this same name, or you will overwrite the sample file.

Creating a Layout

First, start up *Trax*. You will notice that most of the options and buttons are greyed out. This is because we don't yet have a layout to work on. Click File | New and the 'New Layout' dialog box will appear. Enter a size of 18 feet by 3 feet. You can abbreviate feet to ft but you must specify units unless you mean millimetres. *Trax* works internally in mm and assumes all measurements are of this form unless otherwise specified. Click OK, and you should have a nice long layout with 1 ft gridlines on a green background (if we had specified a size in mm or m, the gridlines would be at 500 mm intervals).

The Trax Screen

Now that we have a layout, most of the elements of the Trax screen become active, so we can take a look at them. At the top of the screen are the standard caption and menu bars. Below this, to the left, are a number of Toolbuttons, which provide quicker access than the menu to the more commonly required features of Trax. To the right of this are a series of Palettes. Each Palette provides a number of buttons which enable you to add particular parts to your layout. On the Track Palette are straights, curves, points, crossings, feeds etc. On the Controls Palette are the lever frames, switches, buttons and train controllers. Finally, on the Miscellaneous Palette are labels, rulers and signals.

The main window area is divided into two parts. In the upper part is the layout track plan, and in the lower part is the control panel. You can drag the dividing line between these two up and down so that, for example, when you are working on the track plan, you can minimise the space occupied by the control panel. Finally, along the bottom of the screen is a status bar, which will prompt you from time to time with a message or line of information.

Adding and Joining Track Parts

Now add some track. Click the 'Straight Track' button on the 'Track' palette near the top of the screen and then click the mouse to position three lengths of straight one above the other roughly in the central part of the layout. Next, join them up. On the Track palette, click the Joining tool. Then click one end of the middle straight. It should be highlighted in purple, and the end to be joined indicated by a small cross. If it isn't, you didn't quite click between the rails. This will be our 'fixed' piece of track – the second piece we click will move to join it. Click one end of another piece of straight and note that it 'moves' to join up with the first. Join the third piece to the other two, and you should now have a long line roughly around the middle of the layout

Now add two very simple stations to the ends of the stretch of single line. From the Track palette, add a right and a left–hand point, one near each end of the straight, and connect them up to the straight using the Joining Tool. Take care to click the straight first, and add the points the right way round. We want to arrive at the station and have the choice of two platforms, so the toe end of the point is to be joined to the end of the straight.

Now add platforms. You may find this easier if you zoom in. Click the 'Zoom Rectangle' button and click/drag the mouse over the left–hand six feet or so of the layout. Add another length of straight and join it to the 'straight on' road of the point. It may run over the edge of the layout. Use the Move tool to position the track (click and drag the mouse) so that the straight runs along the centre of the layout, and ends just a little way short of the layout edge.

Using Flexible Track and the Spacer

We now wish to add a second platform, parallel to the first, and joined to the diverging road of the point with an appropriate curve. This is where the Spacer tool and the Flexible Track part come in handy. The Spacer tool is a dummy track part. It doesn't actually contain any track, but it does have two ends, whose relative position is fixed. You can change this distance by right–clicking on the spacer tool and bringing up the 'Properties' box. This will allow you to change the interval between the two tracks to be spaced. It is set by default to the standard spacing between adjacent tracks for the scale and gauge of your layout. Place a Spacer tool, for the moment anywhere on the layout.

Select the Joining tool, then click the end of the platform road and attach the appropriate side of the Spacer, leaving the other arrow where you want to position the second platform. Position a length of Flexible track roughly parallel to the platform, then join it to the spacer using the Joining tool. Join its other end to the diverging road of the point. Note that the dotted lines of the flexible track have been replaced by a straight and a curve of the radius required to fill the gap. You can use flexible track in this way to join any two track ends. Trax will attempt to find a configuration of straights and curves that will do the job. If you make a mistake, and end up with the wrong parts on the layout, you can right click them, and select 'Delete' to get rid of them. Once its purpose has been served, delete the spacer tool.

Repeat the process at the other end of the line. Use Ctrl+Right Arrow to get there. Take care over which way the spacer faces. Remember we are making a mirror image of the first station, so the arrows this time need to face inwards. Return to Full View (Ctrl+Home). You should now have a long single track main line with two very simple stations, which we will call A and B, at either end.

Signalling

Now let us add some signals. Zoom back in to the left hand station (A), click the 'Misc' palette, and select a signal. Position this above the main line, beyond the point. This will be our starter signal. Then position a second signal opposite it, to represent the home signal. You will find this is the wrong way round, so right click it, go into Properties and change the orientation from West to East.

Now try your signals out. Go into Test/Operate mode, by clicking the little green arrow on the Toolbar. You will notice that the track has all gone grey. Grey represents electrically 'dead' track – we have not yet added any controller or feed, so there is no power to the line. However, you will find that the mouse

cursor has turned into a finger, and this can be used to operate the point and signals manually. Experiment with this, then return to 'Design' mode by clicking the green arrow a second time.

Adding Track Feeds and Breaks

We now want to add some power, so go to the 'Controls' palette. The white rectangle below the layout is the control panel, and this is where we want to position our controls. This is easier with a grid, so click Options|Control Panel Snap Grid. Click the Controller button on the palette and position a controller on the control panel, to the left of centre. Position a second controller in a similar position on the right. Note that controllers are automatically colour–coded. Place a Track Feed from the Track palette on the straight between the two signals. Right–click it, then in Properties put 'perm' in the 'Connect to controller 1' box. This specifies a permanent connection.

Now repeat the Test/Operate

procedure and note that we now have red colour–coded track where there is power, and grey where there is not (in the platform road not selected by the point.) However, if you zoom out to a full view, you will see that the red colour–coding extends right into station area B, which is not necessarily what we want. Therefore, we need a break in the track just beyond the feed. Exit Test/Operate mode (you cannot add track parts in this mode) and place a Track Break just beyond the feed. Test again, and you will see that we now have limited the scope of the red controller to station area A only.

Next, zoom in on station B, and repeat the process of adding signals, track feed and break there. Connect the track feed to controller 2 this time, and when you now test the layout in Full View, you should have a red and a green colour–coded scope for the two controllers with a grey dead section of line between them.

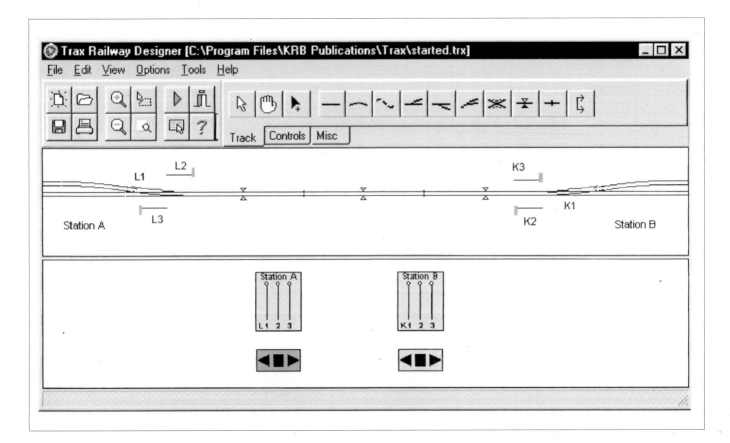

Operating from a Lever Frame

All our signals and points at present are manually operated. We will now automate them, and in the process add some electrical switching to feed power to the 'dead' track at appropriate times. We will adopt the principle that the operator who stops the train will drive it, and use the layout signalling to decide which operator that should be.

Signals and points will be operated by a lever frame, so go to the Controls palette, and select the Lever Frame button. Place a frame above each of the controllers on the control panel, then right–click it, select Properties, and change the number of levers to 3. We only need a lever for the point and two for the signals at each end. You can have up to 100 levers on a single frame if you wish. You may notice that things look a little untidy when you have changed the lever frames. You may have noticed this also if you had to delete any track parts earlier. Trax does not automatically re–draw the whole layout every time the smallest thing changes. It erases and re–draws only the minimum, and sometimes this leaves a little litter behind. You can get rid of this by clicking View|Refresh, or the F5 button on your keyboard.

Now we will assign levers to points and signals. Right click the point in station A and in its Properties dialog, in the 'Setting changed by' box, enter L1. Levers in the first lever frame are called L1, L2, etc. Those in the second, K1, K2 and so on. Go back into test mode and observe that lever L1 now changes our point. You can no longer change it manually, ie by clicking on it. Points and signals are either manual or automated, never both. Assign lever L2 to the outgoing starter signal, and lever L3 to the incoming home signal in the same way. Test that these operate in the way you would expect, then repeat the process for station B, taking care to assign lever K2 to the outgoing signal.

Labelling

You will find it easier to operate the layout if you label the points and signals, so go to the 'Misc' palette, select the Text Label button, and place a label adjacent to A's starter signal. Right–click the label, and in its Properties dialog, give it the caption 'L2' (because it is operated by lever L2). Set its size so that it is easily legible. Note that the size of labels is given in mm, as if they were actually painted on the layout. This is more convenient than using point size, as a legible label at most scales would need to be several hundred points in size. You can adjust the position of the labels using the Move tool. Label the other signals and points with their appropriate lever numbers.

Connecting Power to the Track

Now we wish to feed some power to the central dead section. Position a feed here, go into its Properties dialog, and under 'Connect to controller 1 if' type 'L3'. Similarly connect it to controller 2 if 'K3'. If you now go into Test/Operate mode, you should find that each of the 'incoming' signal levers cause the central section to be assigned to the controller whose home signal is off. If you reverse both signals, you will get a message from Trax, indicating that it has detected an error – the central feed is connected to two controllers, which is not advisable! We should use lever locking to prevent this combination of levers, but at present Trax does not support locking. (This will come in a later version of Trax)

There is still one more step to take. We have a switchable central section, but if we want our two controllers to drive a train all the way from the opposite station, we also need to extend the scope into that station, not just the central section. Therefore, we will introduce a further operating rule for the feeds at the station throats. Right–click the feed in station A, whose connection is at present permanently to controller 1, and change this to controller 1 if 'L2'. The '–' sign is short–hand for NOT, so the feed will be connected to controller 1 unless L2 is pulled. Then, under 'Connect to controller 2' enter the rule 'L2&K3'. Having done

this, repeat the process for the feed in station B, assigning it to controller 1 if 'K2&L3' and to controller 2 if 'K2'.

If you now go into Test/Operate, you should find that the red controller has control of station A, unless the Starter signal (L2) is off. The green controller has control of station B unless K2 is off. When both starter and home signal for a given route are both off, control is with the controller in whose station the train will stop. Once the train has passed the starter signal, it can be returned to danger, and the 'local' controller regains control over the station, whilst the other controller retains the central section. Thus shunting could proceed whilst the train makes its way over to the other station.

This is an extremely simple example, but it illustrates the process of using Trax. The same process would enable you to build up a large layout with multiple controllers and a complex track formation, then test out your wiring logic. Having worked through this example, you could now look at the sample layout files included with your Trax installation.

Some Hints

There are various aspects of Trax that may cause some confusion until you become familiar with them. It is hoped that the following hints will help.

'Read Only' Properties

If you add a Track Part to your layout, for example, a point, then you will normally right–click it and select the switch blade length, crossing angle etc. appropriate to your needs. However, once you have joined this part to any others these properties become read only. You cannot alter them with the Properties box. This is because the geometry of surrounding track parts may be altered if you change, say, a point's crossing angle.

If you need to adjust a part already joined to others, right–click it, then select 'Isolate Part'. This will disconnect it from its neighbours. You can then move it, change it, and rejoin it to its neighbours

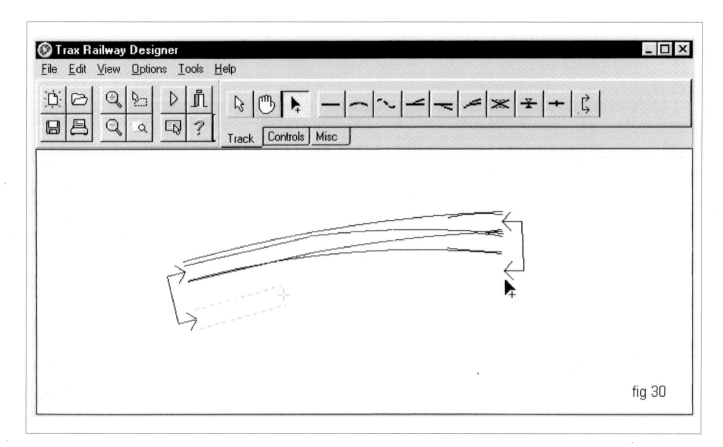

fig 30

in the sequence you require. Properties that do not affect the geometry of adjoining parts can be altered even when a part is connected up.

Lost Curves

If you carry out the above procedure on a curve, you can 'lose' it. Basically, unattached curves are always drawn symmetrically about the 'twelve o'clock' position. Thus, for example, a 60–degree curve would extend from the '11 o'clock' position to the '1 o'clock' position. When you first create a curve, it will be created in this way with the left–hand end where you clicked. If you subsequently attach it to other track parts, it may end up in some completely different orientation. Subsequently, if you Isolate it and change its length or radius, Trax will re–draw it in the '12 o'clock' position, keeping the same centre point. This may take it off the layout. To find it again, simple zoom out (Ctrl+PgDn) until you see it, then use the Move Tool to bring it back onto the layout.

Short Lengths of Track

If you use a length of flexible track to join two ends, one of which is a spacer tool you may on occasion have difficulty trying to join something else onto the end from which you subsequently delete the spacer. Trax will give you an error message saying the end is already joined, when apparently there is nothing attached to it. Invariably this turns out to be a very short length of track, sometimes so short it is not at all visible on the track plan. Where you think you are clicking on an unjoined end, you are in fact selecting the end of a track part already attached to the very short length. The problem is solved if you use the Parts List tool. Select 'Short Lengths' then click 'Update' and Trax will list all lengths less than 1" or 25mm. You can then click on these, press 'Select', and they will be highlighted on the layout track plan. Using the Edit menu, you can look at their Properties, Isolate or Delete them.

Trax will try to avoid short lengths, preferring to increase the length of an existing straight instead. However, when using the spacer tool, this option may not be available to it.

Moving More than You Wanted

The Move Tool may take a little practice. When you select items for editing etc, the current selection normally replaces previous selections. This is not so with the Move Tool. You may wish to select several items, for example a track formation, signals and labels, then move them as a group. To do this, select the Move Tool, then click on each of the items you want to move. You can now click and drag one of them to move them all, as the selections are all still operative.

However, this can give rise to some confusion if you have moved one part, which remains selected, whilst you then move another. You will find that the part you have left selected will move too. To cancel all selections, select Edit|Clear Selection, or hit the 'Esc' key.

Locating feeds and breaks

Every track part has the facility to take a track break at each of its ends, plus one feed (from up to four controllers). The feed is normally in the centre of the part, except for points, where it goes at the toe end as described in Chapter 1. When you click a part to add a break or feed, it will appear in one of these fixed positions. If the positioning of your track break is critical, you should adjust the length of the track part onto which the break is added.

Labels

Label objects will only be drawn as text if they are likely to be legible at the current zoom ratio. Otherwise, they will be drawn as straight lines. The size of a label is defined by the character height in mm as

if it were actually painted on the layout itself, for the reasons already mentioned.

Curved Points

Trax allows you to create curved points, with any angle and radius of turnout and similar or contrary flexure. However it does not at present provide any geometrical support to tell you what radii and angles to use in a given situation. It is planned that a future release will include this support. For the moment, you could adopt the following procedure, for example to make a crossover on a double track curve (you can follow the procedure in sample file 'curved geometry.trx'):

First create a point with the desired outer radius, and an inner radius about 30% less. In the example, we have used 8ft and 5ft. See fig 30.

Using the spacer tool at each end, create the 'inner' track for the crossover. Delete the spacers.

Use the 'inner' curve's radius in the properties box of a second point, and give it an outer curve radius about 25% more.

Attach it temporarily and observe the relative positions of the ends. If you zoom in on the example, you will see that the inner curve needs to be a lot longer before the two turnouts will meet.

Take a guess. In this case, we have given the inner curve an angle of 25°.

Join the two turnout curves with flexible track. You will need to shorten the length of this first.

With the spacer tool and another length of flexible track, complete the outer curve.

Selecting Awkward Parts

Sometimes, it is hard to click on the part you want. Try zooming in – this always makes things easier. However, you may still have difficulty, for example, if you are trying to click on a track break between the diverging roads of two points in a crossover. In this case, use the Parts List, as illustrated in fig 31. Simply double click the name or ID number of the part you want to select and click 'Select Part'. You can then use the Edit menu to change its properties, isolate it, or delete it.

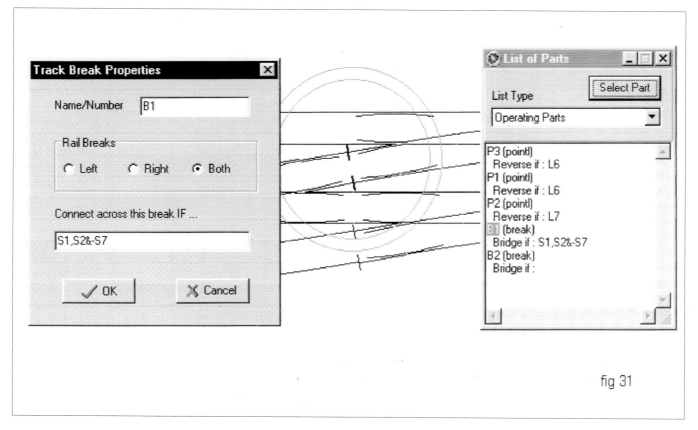

fig 31

APPENDIX

Component Specifications

High Power Transistors

Designation	Type	Vce	Ic	Power	Gain	Case
TIP121	npn	80	5A	60W	1000	TOP66
TIP131	npn	80	12A	70W	1000	TOP66
2N3055	npn	60	15A	115W	45	TO3
MJ3001	npn	80	10A	150W	1000	TO3
TIP127	pnp	100	5A	60W	1000	TOP66
TIP135	pnp	60	12A	70W	1000	TOP66
MJ2955	pnp	60	15A	150W	45	TO3
MJ2501	pnp	80	10A	150W	1000	TO3

Medium Power Transistors

Designation	Type	Vce	Ic	Power	Gain	Case
BFY51	npn	30	1A	800mW	120	TO5
2N3053	npn	40	700mA	800mW	150	TO5
2N2905	pnp	40	600mA	600mW	200	TO5

Low Power Transistors

Designation	Type	Vce	Ic	Power	Gain	Case
BC184C	npn	30	200mA	300mW	450	TO92a
BC109C	npn	20	100mA	300mW	520	TO18
2N3705	npn	30	800mA	360mW	100	TO92
BC178	pnp	25	100mA	300mW	240	TO18
2N3702	pnp	25	200mA	300mW	180	TO92

Diodes

Designation	Type	PIV	I max	Case
1N4148	Single	100	75mA	DO35
1N4001	Single	50	1A	DO41
1N5400	Single	50	3A	DO27
P600	Single	600	6A	P6
W02	Bridge	200v	1.5A	B2
GBPC102	Bridge	200v	3A	B3
KBPC602	Bridge	200v	6A	B4

NOTE

None of the circuits in this book are particularly critical as regards component choice. If you have difficulty in obtaining any of the specific types mentioned, then you can substitute any transistor with at least the same current gain, Ic, Vce and Power rating, or any diode/rectifier with at least the same PIV and I max rating.

SEMICONDUCTOR PINS

*As seen from BELOW

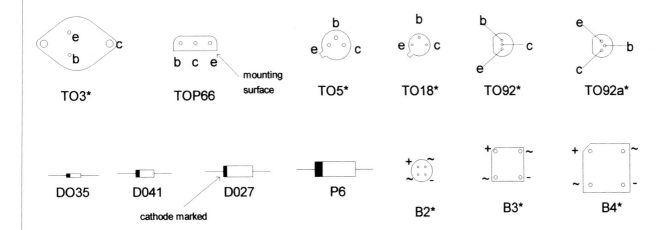

TO3* TOP66 TO5* TO18* TO92* TO92a*

mounting surface

DO35 D041 D027 P6 B2* B3* B4*

cathode marked

RESISTOR COLOUR CODES

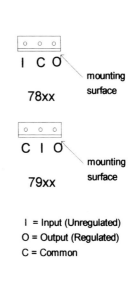

band 1	band 2	band 3	band 4	band 5
1st digit	2nd digit	3rd digit	multiplier	tolerance
0 black	0 black	0 black	x1 black	1% brown
1 brown	1 brown	1 brown	x10 brown	2% red
2 red	2 red	2 red	x100 red	5% gold
3 orange	3 orange	3 orange	x1000 orange	10% silver
4 yellow	4 yellow	4 yellow	x10000 yellow	
5 green	5 green	5 green	x100000 green	
6 blue	6 blue	6 blue	x1000000 blue	
7 purple	7 purple	7 purple		
8 grey	8 grey	8 grey	x0.1 gold	
9 white	9 white	9 white	x0.01 silver	

Note on some resistors, there are only four bands.
In these cases, band 3 is omitted. For example a
resistor coded red, green, black, red, brown is
15k ohms, 1%. The same resistor in the 4-band
scheme would be red, green, orange, brown.

IC PIN CONNECTIONS

I C O

mounting surface

78xx

C I O

mounting surface

79xx

I = Input (Unregulated)
O = Output (Regulated)
C = Common

fig 32

INDEX